Legacy Languages:

Model COBOL programs with logic examples

By Gabriel F. Gargiulo

Introduction

This book is for someone who has the job of programming in COBOL. It contains complete, working, generic programs. They illustrate the major types of business logic that are needed. It is also a complete resource for a training coordinator who is setting up a company's training class in COBOL. In addition, it is a wonderful way to learn a new programming language, if you already know one.

They are generic programs to illustrate programming logic. They were run and tested on an IBM mainframe computer running **z/OS** and **Enterprise COBOL** in October 2020.

A well written program needs two things: good language syntax and good logic. Your COBOL must be good COBOL. Your instructions must be written correctly or they won't do what you want. More important than that is the right approach to solving the problem, the logic.

There are enough books on COBOL language syntax on the market to sink three battleships, and this book does not contain COBOL syntax, but one that I would recommend is *Structured COBOL*, published by Mike Murach Associates.

There are millions of programs now running on business computers. I doubt that any two are exactly the same. But does that mean that they are all totally different? I doubt it. If you looked at all those programs you would probably find that they fall into a few select categories.

This book is about those categories. It contains general solutions to business programming problems. Using these solutions, it should be possible to handle any business programming problem you encounter.

Is programming an art, something that requires a certain in-born talent? Or can it be learned? The right answer is a little bit of each. This book can't help with the in-born talent. It can help by showing you logic solutions that have worked, that have been tried and tested, and have won acceptance in the industry.

I start with the premise that there is a small number of fundamental business programming problems, and that most concrete applications programs will fall into one or possibly a combination of these. This book will show you model programs for these programming tasks.

The logic used in this book is consistent with the logic in use at major corporations (I've worked and taught at more than a few...) It is in essential agreement with the logic in common use. (There may be style differences.) I show you structured COBOL logic that works.

If you are a training coordinator you can use this book to set up a COBOL programming class. All the data files required as input to these programs are on my website shown just below. You will also find there MVS JCL that you can use to define and load the VSAM KSDS data files that are used. It is unlikely that the JCL will work exactly as given: you'll have to modify it for your installation's requirements.

Introduction

This book is an excellent choice for the self-taught programmer. If you have access to a computer system do all the programs that you have time for.

About the line numbers in the first column on the left. Their main purpose is to ensure that the significant code starts in the correct column. (Asterisk for comment in column 7, section and paragraph names in column 8.)

A few words about the style of programming used in this book. Periods are used only where required, after each Data Division entry, after paragraph names, and after the last sentence in each paragraph. Exit paragraphs are not used. Perform THRU is not used. GOBACK is used to end the program. IF is followed by THEN, optional ELSE, END-IF.

If you don't like the use of a one-way transfer of control to ERROR-EXIT, them change it to a PERFORM. The result will be the same.

There are many other program styles that you are likely to see. Many installations require all PERFORMs to be PERFORM THRU. If that is the case, it will be easy to modify these programs for that requirement.

I avoid unnecessary words, such as "TO" in the file assignment statement, and "BLOCK CONTAINS" clauses in the File FDs.

This book does not teach IBM MVS JCL. My book on JCL (out of print) does. Nevertheless, I'll show you sample JCL that you can use with each program. I won't show you a JOB JCL statement however, since that would require knowledge of your company's JCL standards.

This book does not teach MVS/TSO (Time Sharing Option.) My book on TSO (out of print) does that.

You'll find everything you need about VSAM programming with COBOL. But you will have to find out your company's naming conventions and change some file or data set names. You'll have to submit some JCL (shown in this book) to create the VSAM files.

Gabe Gargiulo

Table of Contents

Table of Contents

1. SEQSIMP1. The Simple, Single File Program

SEQSIMP1.

This program reads every record in a file and does some processing with each record read. Our sample program will just write each record out to another file. It will not produce a report, nor will it reformat the records in any way. This is a simple COPY program.

This program basically just copies an input file to an output file. It makes no changes to the file. It does not print anything out or display anything.

Here are some other types of programs that fall into the same logic pattern:
1 a program that simply counts the records in a file
2 a program that copies all the records in a file but has different record descriptions on the input file and output file. That would make this a copy and reformat program
3 a program that copies all the records in one type of file, such as a VSAM file, and writes them out to another type of file, such as an ordinary sequential file.

Here is a short explanation of some of the logic of SEQSIMP1. The logic shown in this program is the kind used in many companies and has become an industry standard.

It starts with the simple PERFORM INITIALIZATION, PERFORM PROCESS-ALL until the end of the file, PERFORM TERMINATION, followed by a GOBACK to end the program.

INITIALIZATION is for those things that are done once at the beginning of the program. PROCESS-ALL is the main controlling loop which does most of the work. TERMINATION is for those things done once at the end of the program.

PROCESS-ALL ends with an unconditional READ - so that READ will be done no matter what happens in PROCESS-ALL. If this READ is skipped for any reason, the program will loop without end. The first part of PROCESS-ALL does the bulk of the program's work. It typically formats output lines and them writes them. Major logic decisions are normally done there, although this program has none.

1. SEQSIMP1. The Simple, Single File Program

The program **SEQSIMP1:**

```
000200 IDENTIFICATION DIVISION.
000300 PROGRAM-ID. SEQSIMP1.
000400* This program just reads an input file and
000500* writes every record to the output file
000600* this is actually a copy program
001000 ENVIRONMENT DIVISION.
001100 CONFIGURATION SECTION.
001200 INPUT-OUTPUT SECTION.
001300 FILE-CONTROL.
001400*  INPUT FILE: PARTS
001500      SELECT IN-FILE  ASSIGN PARTS.
001800*  OUTPUT FILE: SEND TO PRINTER
001900      SELECT OUT-FILE ASSIGN OUTFILE.
002200 DATA DIVISION.
002300 FILE SECTION.
002400 FD  IN-FILE
002410      RECORDING MODE IS F
002700      RECORD CONTAINS 80 CHARACTERS.
003000 01  IN-RECORD.
003010*      PICTURES MUST CORRESPOND TO THE ACTUAL INPUT FILE
003020      05  PART-NUMBER     PIC X(6).
003040      05  filler          pic x.
003050      05  PART-DESC       PIC X(30).
003060      05  filler          pic x.
003070      05  QTY-ON-HAND     PIC 9(3).
003080      05  filler          pic x.
003090      05  QTY-ON-ORDER    PIC 9(3).
003100      05  filler          pic x.
003110      05  QTY-ON-RESERVE  PIC 9(3).
003120      05  filler          pic x.
003130      05  PART-PRICE      PIC 9(3)V99.
003130      05  UNUSED          PIC X(25).
003140
003200 FD  OUT-FILE
003210      RECORDING MODE IS F
003600      RECORD CONTAINS 80 CHARACTERS.
003700 01  OUT-RECORD PIC X(80).
003800
003900 WORKING-STORAGE SECTION.
004000 01  SWITCHES.
004100      05  FILE-AT-END    PIC X  VALUE 'N'.
004200
004300 01  RECORD-COUNT          PIC S9(7) PACKED-DECIMAL VALUE +0.
004400 01  DISPLAY-RECORD-COUNT  PIC Z(6)9.
006000
```

1. SEQSIMP1. The Simple, Single File Program

```
006100 01  WS-OUT-RECORD.
006200     05  OUT-PART-NUMBER     PIC X(6).
006300     05  filler          pic x.
006400     05  OUT-PART-DESC       PIC X(30).
006500     05  filler          pic x.
006600     05  OUT-QTY-ON-HAND     PIC 9(3).
006700     05  filler          pic x.
006800     05  OUT-QTY-ON-ORDER    PIC 9(3).
006900     05  filler          pic x.
007000     05  OUT-QTY-ON-RESERVE  PIC 9(3).
007100     05  filler          pic x.
007200     05  OUT-PART-PRICE      PIC 9(3)V99.
007300     05  OUT-UNUSED          PIC X(25).
007400
007500 PROCEDURE DIVISION.
007700**    perform beginning, perform main loop til no more records,
007800**    perform the end
007900**    please note the style of using periods
008000**    only before and after paragraph names
008100**    and at physical end of program.
008200     PERFORM INITIALIZATION
008300     PERFORM PROCESS-ALL
008400**        UPPER CASE Y, PLEASE
008500         UNTIL FILE-AT-END = 'Y'
008600     PERFORM TERMINATION
008700     GOBACK.
008800
008900 INITIALIZATION.
009000*    In this part you do the things you need to do once only
009100*    at the beginning of the program
009200*    please read the first record! This logic depends on it
009300     OPEN INPUT IN-FILE
009400         OUTPUT OUT-FILE
009500     PERFORM READ-PAR.
009600
009700 PROCESS-ALL.
009800*    This is performed once for each record read
009900*    it is the most important part of the program
010000*    you generally do three things:
010100*      process input record and/ or format output record
010200*      write the output record
010300*      read next input record (don't forget this)
010400*    formatting the output record:
010800     MOVE PART-NUMBER      TO OUT-PART-NUMBER
010900     MOVE PART-DESC        TO OUT-PART-DESC
011000     MOVE QTY-ON-HAND      TO OUT-QTY-ON-HAND
011100     MOVE QTY-ON-ORDER     TO OUT-QTY-ON-ORDER
011200     MOVE QTY-ON-RESERVE   TO OUT-QTY-ON-RESERVE
011300     MOVE PART-PRICE       TO OUT-PART-PRICE
011400     MOVE UNUSED           TO OUT-UNUSED
011500*    I have adopted the style of the write from
011700*    because it would be awkward to write different types of
011800*    print lines if you didn't do a write from
011900*    this will be more obvious in programs that do reports
012000     WRITE OUT-RECORD      FROM WS-OUT-RECORD
012100     PERFORM READ-PAR.
```

1. SEQSIMP1. The Simple, Single File Program

```
012300 TERMINATION.
012400*    Here you do what you need to do once only
012500*    after all records have been processed
012600*    and you are ready to end
012700*    this might include final totals, for example
012800*    move record-count to display-record-count
012900*    display puts the data item directly to the printer
013000*    DISPLAY DISPLAY-RECORD-COUNT
013100     CLOSE IN-FILE OUT-FILE.
013200
013300 READ-PAR.
013600     READ IN-FILE
013700         AT END MOVE 'Y' TO FILE-AT-END
013800*        I included the code to count input records
013900*        although it is commented out
014000*        not at end add 1 to record-count
014100     END-READ.
```

1. SEQSIMP1. The Simple, Single File Program

The input data file **PARTS**: (the next two lines are a column ruler)

```
         1         2         3         4         5         6
123456789.123456789.123456789.123456789.123456789.123456789.12345678

PART01 LEFT HANDED WIDGET WRENCHES    003 007 002 10022
PART02 LEAD-WINGED GLIDERS            004 006 001 14054
PART04 LEFT FOOT REEBOKS              021 002 004 04323
PART06 286 COMPUTERS W 4K HARD DISK   043 077 012 00042
```

Here is sample JCL:

```
//STEP1     EXEC PGM=SEQSIMP1
//STEPLIB DD DSN=your.executable.program.library.here,DISP=SHR
//*   THE NEXT LIBRARY NAME MAY BE DIFFERENT AT YOUR CO.
//PARTS     DD    DSN=userid.COBBOOK.DATA(PARTS),DISP=SHR
//OUTFILE   DD    SYSOUT=*
//SYSOUT    DD    SYSOUT=*
//SYSUDUMP  DD    SYSOUT=*
```

Expected output:
```
PART01 LEFT HANDED WIDGET WRENCHES    003 007 002 10022
PART02 LEAD-WINGED GLIDERS            004 006 001 14054
PART04 LEFT FOOT REEBOKS              021 002 004 04323
PART06 286 COMPUTERS W 4K HARD DISK   043 077 012 00042
```

1. SEQSIMP1. The Simple, Single File Program

This page intentionally left blank

2. SEQRPT1. The Simple, Single File Report Program

SEQRPT1.

Same as the Simple, Single File Program, #1 above, but it prints things on paper, producing a report. It will print each record that it reads (detail printing) Also, some printing logic is needed in order to print out headers and detail lines. Logic is needed to change the page when needed.

This type of program is very common. It simply reports on what is found in a file, formatting it in a way that is easy to read. Although the major logic path is not complex, it may be combined with a **table lookup** which will transform some value found on the file into some other, more meaningful value for use on the report.

Here is an explanation of the logic of SEQRPT1. This program's logic is very similar to that of SEQSIMP1, but it prints out a report, so there is output formatting, lines are counted, (end of paragraph PROCESS-ALL) so that the page can be changed at the appropriate time (first thing in paragraph PROCESS-ALL.)

All WRITE statements have an added option - AFTER ADVANCING. This causes the compiler to take on the job of controlling printer spacing (end of paragraph HEADING-ROUTINE). PAGE makes it go to the top of the next page, 1 LINE advances 1 line, etc. Please use AFTER ADVANCING only with report files, do not use it with data files that will normally be read only by another program.

AFTER ADVANCING steals the first character of your print line, using it for printer control commands, so you can't use it for anything else.

2. SEQRPT1. The Simple, Single File Report Program

The program **SEQRPT1:**

```
000200 IDENTIFICATION DIVISION.
000300 PROGRAM-ID. SEQRPT1.
000400*    General logic for program that reads every input record
000500*     and then prints it out.
000600* header and detail line, page change
000700 ENVIRONMENT DIVISION.
000800 CONFIGURATION SECTION.
000900 INPUT-OUTPUT SECTION.
001000 FILE-CONTROL.
001100*    INPUT FILE PARTS
001200       SELECT IN-FILE  ASSIGN PARTS.
001500*    OUTPUT FILE: SEND TO PRINTER
001600       SELECT OUT-FILE ASSIGN OUTFILE.
001900 DATA DIVISION.
002000 FILE SECTION.
002100 FD  IN-FILE
002110     RECORDING MODE IS F
002500     RECORD CONTAINS 80 CHARACTERS.
002600 01  IN-RECORD.
002610     05  PART-NUMBER     PIC X(6).
002620     05  filler          pic x.
002630     05  PART-DESC       PIC X(30).
002640     05  filler          pic x.
002650     05  QTY-ON-HAND     PIC 9(3).
002660     05  filler          pic x.
002670     05  QTY-ON-ORDER    PIC 9(3).
002680     05  filler          pic x.
002690     05  QTY-ON-RESERVE  PIC 9(3).
002700     05  filler          pic x.
002710     05  PART-PRICE      PIC 9(3)V99.
002720     05  UNUSED          PIC X(25).
002730
002800 FD  OUT-FILE
002810     RECORDING MODE IS F
003000* Record length can be more than input file
003100* because you are printing, not copying to a file
003400     RECORD CONTAINS 133 CHARACTERS.
003500 01  OUT-RECORD PIC X(133).
003600
003700 WORKING-STORAGE SECTION.
003800 01  SWITCHES.
003900     05  FILE-AT-END     PIC X  VALUE 'N'.
004000
004100 01  COUNTERS-AND-ACCUMULATORS.
004200     05  LINES-PRINTED        PIC S9(5)
004300          PACKED-DECIMAL VALUE 0.
004400     05  INPUT-RECORD-COUNT   PIC S9(5)
004500          PACKED-DECIMAL VALUE 0.
004600     05  OUTPUT-RECORD-COUNT  PIC S9(5)
004700          PACKED-DECIMAL VALUE 0.
004800*    55 is a very common value. use more or less according
004900*    to your program's requirements
005000     05  MAX-PER-PAGE         PIC S9(5) PACKED-DECIMAL
005100          VALUE +55.
006700
```

2. SEQRPT1. The Simple, Single File Report Program

```
006800 01  WS-OUT-RECORD.
006900*   We will use edit fields for the numeric fields
007000*   we are using fillers between the fields for legibility
007100     05   FILLER                 PIC X(3) VALUE SPACES.
007200     05   OUT-PART-NUMBER        PIC X(6).
007300     05   FILLER                 PIC X(3) VALUE SPACES.
007400     05   OUT-PART-DESC          PIC X(30).
007500     05   FILLER                 PIC X(3) VALUE SPACES.
007600     05   OUT-QTY-ON-HAND        PIC ZZ9.
007700     05   FILLER                 PIC X(3) VALUE SPACES.
007800     05   OUT-QTY-ON-ORDER       PIC ZZ9.
007900     05   FILLER                 PIC X(3) VALUE SPACES.
008000     05   OUT-QTY-ON-RESERVE     PIC ZZ9.
008100     05   FILLER                 PIC X(3) VALUE SPACES.
008200     05   OUT-PART-PRICE         PIC ZZZ.99.
008300     05   FILLER                 PIC X(3) VALUE SPACES.
008400     05   OUT-UNUSED             PIC X(30).
008500     05   FILLER                 PIC X(31) VALUE SPACES.
008600
008700 01  HEADER-1.
008800*     Leave first character position blank
008900*      because of after advancing
009000     05   FILLER                 PIC X VALUE SPACE.
009100     05   FILLER                 PIC X(80)
009200          VALUE 'PRINT OF DATA FILE FOR ABC COMPANY'.
009300
009400 PROCEDURE DIVISION.
009500     PERFORM INITIALIZATION
009600*     UPPER CASE Y, PLEASE
009700     PERFORM PROCESS-ALL
009800          UNTIL FILE-AT-END = 'Y'
009900     PERFORM TERMINATION
010000     GOBACK.
010100
010200 INITIALIZATION.
010300     OPEN INPUT IN-FILE
010400          OUTPUT OUT-FILE
010500     PERFORM HEADING-ROUTINE
010600     PERFORM READ-PAR.
010700
010800 PROCESS-ALL.
010900     IF LINES-PRINTED > MAX-PER-PAGE
011000     THEN
011100          PERFORM HEADING-ROUTINE
011200     END-IF
011300     MOVE PART-NUMBER     TO OUT-PART-NUMBER
011400     MOVE PART-DESC       TO OUT-PART-DESC
011500     MOVE QTY-ON-HAND     TO OUT-QTY-ON-HAND
011600     MOVE QTY-ON-ORDER    TO OUT-QTY-ON-ORDER
011700     MOVE QTY-ON-RESERVE  TO OUT-QTY-ON-RESERVE
011800     MOVE PART-PRICE      TO OUT-PART-PRICE
011900     MOVE UNUSED          TO OUT-UNUSED
012000     WRITE OUT-RECORD     FROM WS-OUT-RECORD
012100          AFTER ADVANCING 1 LINE
012200     ADD 1 TO LINES-PRINTED
012300     PERFORM READ-PAR.
012400
012500 TERMINATION.
012600     CLOSE IN-FILE OUT-FILE.
```

2. SEQRPT1. The Simple, Single File Report Program

```
012700
012800 READ-PAR.
012900      READ IN-FILE
013000          AT END MOVE 'Y' TO FILE-AT-END
013100      END-READ.
013200
013300 HEADING-ROUTINE.
013400*      after advancing PAGE does a page eject,
013500*      puts printer at top of page
013600*      after doing advancing page,
013700*      all your writes for that file must use the adv. option
013800*      and you must have a blank filler in the first
013900*      character position of the line to be printed
014000      WRITE OUT-RECORD FROM HEADER-1 AFTER ADVANCING PAGE
014100      MOVE 0 TO LINES-PRINTED.
```

The input data file **PARTS**: (the next two lines are a column ruler)

```
          1         2         3         4         5         6
123456789.123456789.123456789.123456789.123456789.123456789.12345678

PART01 LEFT HANDED WIDGET WRENCHES      003 007 002 10022
PART02 LEAD-WINGED GLIDERS              004 006 001 14054
PART04 LEFT FOOT REEBOKS                021 002 004 04323
PART06 286 COMPUTERS W 4K HARD DISK     043 077 012 00042
```

Here is sample JCL:

```
//STEP1     EXEC PGM=SEQRPT1
//STEPLIB DD DSN=your.executable.program.library.here,DISP=SHR
//*   THE NEXT LIBRARY NAME MAY BE DIFFERENT AT YOUR CO
//PARTS     DD   DSN=userid.COBBOOK.DATA(PARTS),DISP=SHR
//OUTFILE   DD   SYSOUT=*
//SYSOUT    DD   SYSOUT=*
//SYSUDUMP  DD   SYSOUT=*
```

Expected output:
```
PRINT OF DATA FILE FOR ABC COMPANY
   PART01    LEFT HANDED WIDGET WRENCHES      3    7    2   100.22
   PART02    LEAD-WINGED GLIDERS              4    6    1   140.54
   PART04    LEFT FOOT REEBOKS               21    2    4    43.23
   PART06    286 COMPUTERS W 4K HARD DISK    43   77   12     .42
```

3. SEQRPT2. The Simple, Single File Report Program with Record Count or Final Totals

SEQRPT2.

Same as The Simple, Single File Report Program, #2 above, but also counts records, or accumulates totals. Then at the end of the file, it prints a record count or total of some money amount.

This type of program may not sound very difficult. It is not. But it is extremely useful: it is the meat and potatoes of many businesses. It absolutely *must* be accurate: It prints out in clear usable form the entire business' or business application's records. Final or grand totals answer the questions: "How much did we produce last year?", "What is the bottom line? "

3. SEQRPT2. The Simple, Single File Report Program with Record Count or Final Totals

The program **SEQRPT2:**

```
000200 IDENTIFICATION DIVISION.
000300 PROGRAM-ID. SEQRPT2.
000400* Read and print every record
000500* header line, detail line, page change, final total
000600* & rec count
000700 ENVIRONMENT DIVISION.
000800 CONFIGURATION SECTION.
000900 INPUT-OUTPUT SECTION.
001000 FILE-CONTROL.
001100*     INPUT FILE: PARTS
001200      SELECT IN-FILE  ASSIGN PARTS.
001500*     OUTFILE: SEND TO PRINTER
001600      SELECT OUT-FILE ASSIGN OUTFILE.
001900 DATA DIVISION.
002000 FILE SECTION.
002100 FD  IN-FILE
002110      RECORDING MODE IS F
002500      RECORD CONTAINS 80 CHARACTERS.
002600 01  IN-RECORD.
002610      05  PART-NUMBER     PIC X(6).
002620      05  filler          pic x.
002630      05  PART-DESC       PIC X(30).
002640      05  filler          pic x.
002650      05  QTY-ON-HAND     PIC 9(3).
002660      05  filler          pic x.
002670      05  QTY-ON-ORDER    PIC 9(3).
002680      05  filler          pic x.
002690      05  QTY-ON-RESERVE  PIC 9(3).
002700      05  filler          pic x.
002710      05  PART-PRICE      PIC 9(3)V99.
002720      05  UNUSED          PIC X(25).
002730
002800 FD  OUT-FILE
002810      RECORDING MODE IS F
003000*     Record length can be more than input file
003100*     because you are printing, not copying to a file
003200      RECORD CONTAINS 133 CHARACTERS.
003500 01  OUT-RECORD PIC X(133).
003600
```

3. SEQRPT2. The Simple, Single File Report Program with Record Count or Final Totals

```
003700 WORKING-STORAGE SECTION.
003800 01   SWITCHES.
003900       05  FILE-AT-END      PIC X  VALUE 'N'.
004000 01   COUNTERS-AND-ACCUMULATORS.
004100       05  LINES-PRINTED         PIC S9(5) PACKED-DECIMAL
004200           VALUE ZERO.
004300       05  INPUT-RECORD-COUNT    PIC S9(5) PACKED-DECIMAL
004400           VALUE ZERO.
004500       05  TOTAL-QUANTITY        PIC S9(7) PACKED-DECIMAL
004600           VALUE ZERO.
004700       05  OUTPUT-RECORD-COUNT   PIC S9(5) PACKED-DECIMAL
004800           VALUE ZERO.
004900       05  MAX-PER-PAGE          PIC S9(5) PACKED-DECIMAL
005000           VALUE +55.
005100
006600 01   WS-OUT-RECORD.
006620*   Using edit fields for the numeric fields
006630*   and fillers between the fields for legibility
006900*      Leave first character position blank
007000*       because of after advancing
007100       05  FILLER            PIC X(3) VALUE SPACES.
007200       05  OUT-PART-NUMBER   PIC X(6).
007300       05  FILLER            PIC X(3) VALUE SPACES.
007400       05  OUT-PART-DESC     PIC X(30).
007500       05  FILLER            PIC X(3) VALUE SPACES.
007600       05  OUT-QTY-ON-HAND   PIC ZZ9.
007700       05  FILLER            PIC X(3) VALUE SPACES.
007800       05  OUT-QTY-ON-ORDER  PIC ZZ9.
007900       05  FILLER            PIC X(3) VALUE SPACES.
008000       05  OUT-QTY-ON-RESERVE PIC ZZ9.
008100       05  FILLER            PIC X(3) VALUE SPACES.
008200       05  OUT-PART-PRICE    PIC ZZZ.99.
008300       05  FILLER            PIC X(3) VALUE SPACES.
008400       05  OUT-UNUSED        PIC X(30).
008500       05  FILLER            PIC X(31) VALUE SPACES.
008600
008700 01   HEADER-1.
008800*      Leave first character position blank
008900*       because of after advancing
009000       05  FILLER            PIC X VALUE SPACE.
009100       05  FILLER            PIC X(80)
009200           VALUE 'PRINT OF DATA FILE FOR ABC COMPANY'.
009300
009400 01   FINAL-TOTAL-LINE.
009500*      LEAVE FIRST CHARACTER POSITION BLANK
009600*       BECAUSE OF AFTER ADVANCING
009700       05  FILLER                    PIC X VALUE SPACE.
009800       05  FILLER                    PIC X(20)
009900           VALUE 'TOTAL QUANTITY '.
010000       05  FILLER                    PIC X VALUE SPACE.
010100       05  PRINT-TOTAL-QUANTITY      PIC Z(7)-.
010200       05  FILLER                    PIC X(20)
010300           VALUE '  RECORDS READ '.
010400       05  FILLER                    PIC X VALUE SPACE.
010500       05  PRINT-INPUT-RECORD-COUNT  PIC Z(7)-.
```

3. SEQRPT2. The Simple, Single File Report Program with Record Count or Final Totals

```
010700 PROCEDURE DIVISION.
010800     PERFORM INITIALIZATION
010900*    UPPER CASE Y
011000     PERFORM PROCESS-ALL
011100         UNTIL FILE-AT-END = 'Y'
011200     PERFORM TERMINATION
011300     GOBACK.
011400
011500 INITIALIZATION.
011600     OPEN INPUT IN-FILE
011700          OUTPUT OUT-FILE
011800     PERFORM HEADING-ROUTINE
011900     PERFORM READ-PAR.
012000
012100 PROCESS-ALL.
012200     IF LINES-PRINTED > MAX-PER-PAGE
012300     THEN
012400         PERFORM HEADING-ROUTINE
012500     END-IF
012600     ADD QTY-ON-HAND      TO TOTAL-QUANTITY
012700     MOVE PART-NUMBER      TO OUT-PART-NUMBER
012800     MOVE PART-DESC        TO OUT-PART-DESC
012900     MOVE QTY-ON-HAND      TO OUT-QTY-ON-HAND
013000     MOVE QTY-ON-ORDER     TO OUT-QTY-ON-ORDER
013100     MOVE QTY-ON-RESERVE TO OUT-QTY-ON-RESERVE
013200     MOVE PART-PRICE       TO OUT-PART-PRICE
013300     MOVE UNUSED           TO OUT-UNUSED
013400     WRITE OUT-RECORD      FROM WS-OUT-RECORD
013500         AFTER ADVANCING 1 LINE
013600     ADD 1 TO OUTPUT-RECORD-COUNT
013700     ADD 1 TO LINES-PRINTED
013800     PERFORM READ-PAR.
013900
014000 TERMINATION.
014100     MOVE TOTAL-QUANTITY  TO PRINT-TOTAL-QUANTITY
014200     MOVE INPUT-RECORD-COUNT TO PRINT-INPUT-RECORD-COUNT
014300     WRITE OUT-RECORD FROM FINAL-TOTAL-LINE
014400         AFTER ADVANCING 5 LINES
014500     CLOSE IN-FILE OUT-FILE.
014600
014700 READ-PAR.
014800     READ IN-FILE
014900         AT END MOVE 'Y' TO FILE-AT-END
015000         NOT AT END ADD 1 TO INPUT-RECORD-COUNT
015100     END-READ.
015300 HEADING-ROUTINE.
015400     WRITE OUT-RECORD FROM HEADER-1 AFTER ADVANCING PAGE
015500     MOVE 0 TO LINES-PRINTED.
```

3. SEQRPT2. The Simple, Single File Report Program with Record Count or Final Totals

The input data file **PARTS**: (the next two lines are a column ruler)

```
         1         2         3         4         5         6
123456789.123456789.123456789.123456789.123456789.123456789.12345678

PART01 LEFT HANDED WIDGET WRENCHES    003 007 002 10022
PART02 LEAD-WINGED GLIDERS            004 006 001 14054
PART04 LEFT FOOT REEBOKS              021 002 004 04323
PART06 286 COMPUTERS W 4K HARD DISK   043 077 012 00042
```

Here is sample JCL:

```
//STEP1    EXEC PGM=SEQRPT2
//STEPLIB DD DSN=your.executable.program.library.here,DISP=SHR
//*  THE NEXT LIBRARY NAME MAY BE DIFFERENT AT YOUR CO
//PARTS    DD   DSN=userid.COBBOOK.DATA(PARTS),DISP=SHR
//OUTFILE  DD   SYSOUT=*
//SYSOUT   DD   SYSOUT=*
//SYSUDUMP DD   SYSOUT=*
```

Expected output:
```
PRINT OF DATA FILE FOR ABC COMPANY
    PART01    LEFT HANDED WIDGET WRENCHES       3     7     2    100.22
    PART02    LEAD-WINGED GLIDERS               4     6     1    140.54
    PART04    LEFT FOOT REEBOKS                21     2     4     43.23
    PART06    286 COMPUTERS W 4K HARD DISK     43    77    12       .42

 TOTAL QUANTITY              71    RECORDS READ            4
```

3. SEQRPT2. The Simple, Single File Report Program with Record Count or Final Totals

This page intentionally left blank

4. SEQCK1. The Sequence Check Program

SEQCK1.
Similar to The Simple, Single File Report Program with record count or final totals, #3 above, but checks the input file to determine whether the records are in sort order on some field, such as an account number. When a record is encountered that is out of order, it prints out the offending record and as much other useful information as possible. At the end of the file, it prints out a record count and the count of records that were out of sequence. If some were out of sequence, it prints out or displays a noticeable error message.

One day this will be your programming assignment:
A file is received from a distant location, from another company, from another business application system within the company. The file should be in sorted order - but what if it isn't? That could cause a database load, a VSAM KSDS load, a file update program or a subtotal program to abend or worse - produce disastrous results. Your job is to write a program that simply checks the sequence of the records.

A few words about the logic of this program. It builds on the logic of the SEQSIMP1 program. However, it must save the field you are checking for sequence, right after reading the first record (in the INITIALIZATION paragraph).

The actual sequence checking is done in a separate paragraph so as to keep PROCESS-ALL simple.

The program makes a major decision (middle of PROCESS-ALL paragraph), whether to write to the valid file or the invalid file.

You may want to call an abend routine in the paragraph ERROR-EXIT to terminate the program with a noticeable message and error code.

4. SEQCK1. The Sequence Check Program

The program **SEQCK1:**

```
000200 IDENTIFICATION DIVISION.
000300* Batch cobol sequence check file
000400 program-id. Seqck1.
000500* logic for program that reads every input record
000600* it writes it out to an output file only if in sequence.
000700* displays a message if records not in sequence
000800 ENVIRONMENT DIVISION.
000900 INPUT-OUTPUT SECTION.
001000 FILE-CONTROL.
001100* Input file: (first time you run it) emp
001200*    (no out of seq records)
001300*    run it a second time with emp1 (out of seq records)
001400      SELECT INPUT-FILE ASSIGN EMP.
001700* Output file:  validfi:
001800*    send to printer for this example.
001900*    in real life it might be a real disk/tape file
002000      SELECT VALID-FILE  ASSIGN VALIDFI.
002300* Output file:  reportfi: a report file,
002400*    prints out information on out of sequence records,
002500*    send to printer
002600      SELECT REPORT-FILE  ASSIGN REPORTFI.
002900
003000 DATA DIVISION.
003100 FILE SECTION.
003200
```

4. SEQCK1. The Sequence Check Program

```
003300 FD  INPUT-FILE
003400     RECORDING MODE IS F
003700     RECORD CONTAINS 80 CHARACTERS.
003710 01  EMPLOYEE-RECORD.
003720     05  FILLER                        PIC X(8).
003730     05  FILLER                        PIC X(01).
003740     05  ER-EMPLOYEE-NUMBER            PIC X(05).
003750     05  FILLER                        PIC X(01).
003760     05  ER-EMPLOYEE-NAME              PIC X(25).
003770     05  FILLER                        PIC X(01).
003780     05  ER-EMPLOYEE-DEPARTMENT        PIC X(05).
003790     05  FILLER                        PIC X(01).
003800     05  ER-EMPLOYEE-SALARY-CODE       PIC X(02).
003810     05  FILLER                        PIC X(01).
003820     05  FILLER                        PIC X(30).
003900
004000 FD  VALID-FILE
004100     RECORDING MODE IS F
004400     RECORD CONTAINS 80 CHARACTERS.
004500 01  VALID-RECORD                      PIC X(80).
004600
004700 FD  REPORT-FILE
004800     RECORDING MODE IS F
005100     RECORD CONTAINS 133 CHARACTERS.
005200
005300 01  REPORT-RECORD                     PIC X(133).
005400
005500 WORKING-STORAGE SECTION.
005600
005700 01  FILE-AT-END        PIC X VALUE 'N'.
005800*
005900 01  SW-VALID-RECORD    PIC X VALUE 'Y'.
006000
007700 01  HOLD-EMPLOYEE-NUMBER   PIC X(5) VALUE SPACES.
007800
007900 01  COUNTERS-AND-ACCUMULATORS.
008000     05  CTR-OUT-OF-SEQ     PIC  S9(5)
008100            PACKED-DECIMAL      VALUE 0.
008200     05  CTR-RECORDS-READ   PIC  S9(5)
008300            PACKED-DECIMAL      VALUE 0.
008400     05  CTR-RECORDS-WRITTEN PIC  S9(5)
008500            PACKED-DECIMAL      VALUE 0.
008600
008700 01  TITLE-HEADING-LINE.
008800     05  FILLER             PIC X(1) VALUE SPACES.
008900     05  FILLER             PIC X(35)
009000                 VALUE 'SEQUENCE CHECK PROGRAM'.
009100     05  FILLER             PIC X(04) VALUE SPACES.
009200     05  FILLER             PIC X(33)
009300                 VALUE 'OUT OF SEQUENCE RECORDS '.
009400     05  REPORT-DATE.
009500         10  REPORT-YY          PIC 99.
009600         10  REPORT-MM          PIC 99.
009700         10  REPORT-DD          PIC 99.
009800
009900 01  DETAIL-INVALID-LINE.
010000     05  FILLER             PIC X(1)  VALUE SPACE.
010100     05  REASON-INVALID     PIC X(30) VALUE SPACES.
010200     05  RECORD-IMAGE       PIC X(80) VALUE SPACES.
010300
```

4. SEQCK1. The Sequence Check Program

```
010400 PROCEDURE DIVISION.
010500     PERFORM INITIALIZATION
010600     PERFORM PROCESS-ALL UNTIL
010700         FILE-AT-END = 'Y'
010800     PERFORM TERMINATION
010900     GOBACK.
011000
011100 INITIALIZATION.
011200     OPEN INPUT INPUT-FILE
011300         OUTPUT VALID-FILE
011400                REPORT-FILE
011500     WRITE REPORT-RECORD FROM TITLE-HEADING-LINE
011600     PERFORM READ-PAR
011700
011800     MOVE ER-EMPLOYEE-NUMBER TO HOLD-EMPLOYEE-NUMBER
011900     ACCEPT REPORT-DATE FROM DATE.
012000
012100 PROCESS-ALL.
012200     MOVE SPACES TO DETAIL-INVALID-LINE
012300     MOVE 'Y' TO SW-VALID-RECORD
012400     PERFORM SEQUENCE-CHECK
012500     IF SW-VALID-RECORD = 'Y'
012600     THEN
012700        PERFORM WRITE-VALID-RECORD
012800        ADD 1 TO CTR-RECORDS-WRITTEN
012900     ELSE
013000        PERFORM PRINT-INVALID-LINE
013100        ADD 1 TO CTR-OUT-OF-SEQ
013200     END-IF
013300
013400     PERFORM READ-PAR.
013500
013600 WRITE-VALID-RECORD.
013700
013800     WRITE VALID-RECORD FROM EMPLOYEE-RECORD.
013900
014000 PRINT-INVALID-LINE.
014100     MOVE EMPLOYEE-RECORD TO RECORD-IMAGE
014200     WRITE REPORT-RECORD FROM DETAIL-INVALID-LINE.
014300
014400 TERMINATION.
014500
014600     CLOSE INPUT-FILE
014700           VALID-FILE
014800           REPORT-FILE
014900     IF CTR-OUT-OF-SEQ > 1
015000     THEN
015100        GO TO ERROR-EXIT.
015200
015300 SEQUENCE-CHECK.
015400     IF ER-EMPLOYEE-NUMBER < HOLD-EMPLOYEE-NUMBER
015500        MOVE    'RECORD OUT OF SEQUENCE (EMPLOYEE-NUMBER)'
015600                TO REASON-INVALID
015700        MOVE    EMPLOYEE-RECORD TO RECORD-IMAGE
015800        MOVE 'N' TO SW-VALID-RECORD
015900        ADD 1 TO CTR-OUT-OF-SEQ
016000     END-IF
016100     MOVE ER-EMPLOYEE-NUMBER TO HOLD-EMPLOYEE-NUMBER.
016200
```

4. SEQCK1. The Sequence Check Program

```
016300   READ-PAR.
016400      READ INPUT-FILE
016500      AT END
016600         MOVE 'Y' TO FILE-AT-END
016700      NOT AT END
016800         ADD 1 TO CTR-RECORDS-READ
016900      END-READ.
017000
017100   ERROR-EXIT.
017200      CLOSE INPUT-FILE
017300            VALID-FILE
017400               REPORT-FILE
017500      DISPLAY 'THERE WERE OUT-OF-SEQUENCE RECORDS'
017600      DISPLAY 'THE OUTPUT FILE MAY NOT BE USEABLE'
017700      GOBACK.
```

The input data file **EMP**: (the next two lines are a column ruler)

```
         1         2         3         4         5         6
123456789.123456789.123456789.123456789.123456789.123456789.12345678

         01000  PEARLE E GATES           D0001 01
         02000  LED BALOON               D0002 04
         03000  ORTIZ, DAVID             D0005 06
         04000  JOE JONES                D0504 01
```

Here is sample JCL:

```
//STEP1     EXEC PGM=SEQCK1
//STEPLIB DD DSN=your.executable.program.library.here,DISP=SHR
//*   THE NEXT LIBRARY NAME MAY BE DIFFERENT AT YOUR CO
//EMP       DD   DSN=userid.COBBOOK.DATA(EMP),DISP=SHR
//VALIDFI   DD   SYSOUT=*
//REPORTFI  DD   SYSOUT=*
//SYSOUT    DD   SYSOUT=*
//SYSUDUMP  DD   SYSOUT=*
```

Expected output:

```
         01000  PEARLE E GATES           D0001 01
         02000  LED BALOON               D0002 04
         03000  ORTIZ, DAVID             D0005 06
         04000  JOE JONES                D0504 01
  SEQUENCE CHECK PROGRAM                 OUT OF SEQUENCE RECORDS
```

4. SEQCK1. The Sequence Check Program

This page intentionally left blank

5. SELECT1. The Record Selection Program.

SELECT1.
Similar to The Simple, Single File Program, #1 above, but writes out only some of the records read. Based on edit criteria, it decides whether to write out a given record or whether to ignore it.

This is a very useful type of program in the business world. Some similar programs might be the following:

All the salespersons' sales are on one huge file. All you need are the salespeople for the Boston district. So, you write a program to pick off only the records containing information on Boston people. It will be much easier to work with the smaller file.

A record selection, or extract program.

Perhaps you need a file that consists of one-tenth the records of the complete file. You would write a program that reads every record, counts them, and writes out only each tenth record.

5. SELECT1. The Record Selection Program.

The program **SELECT1:**

```
000200 IDENTIFICATION DIVISION.
000300*  Select records:
000400*  determine if records should be written to the output file
000500 PROGRAM-ID. SELECT1.
000600 ENVIRONMENT DIVISION.
000700 INPUT-OUTPUT SECTION.
000800 FILE-CONTROL.
000900*    INPUT FILE EMP
001000     SELECT INPUT-FILE ASSIGN EMP.
001300*    OUTPUT FILE NORMALLY A DISK/TAPE FILE,
001400*    BUT IS ASSIGNED TO PRINTER IN THE JCL
001500     SELECT GOOD-FILE ASSIGN GOODFI.
001800
001900 DATA DIVISION.
002000 FILE SECTION.
002100
002200 FD  INPUT-FILE
002300     RECORDING MODE IS F
002600     RECORD CONTAINS 80 CHARACTERS.
002610 01  EMPLOYEE-RECORD.
002620     05  FILLER                    PIC X(8).
002630     05  FILLER                    PIC X(01).
002640     05  ER-EMPLOYEE-NUMBER        PIC X(05).
002650     05  FILLER                    PIC X(01).
002660     05  ER-EMPLOYEE-NAME          PIC X(25).
002670     05  FILLER                    PIC X(01).
002680     05  ER-EMPLOYEE-DEPARTMENT    PIC X(05).
002690     05  FILLER                    PIC X(01).
002700     05  ER-EMPLOYEE-SALARY-CODE   PIC X(02).
002720     05  FILLER                    PIC X(31).
002800
002900 FD  GOOD-FILE
003000     RECORDING MODE IS F
003300     RECORD CONTAINS 80 CHARACTERS.
003400 01  GOOD-RECORD                    PIC X(80).
003500
```

5. SELECT1. The Record Selection Program.

```
003600 WORKING-STORAGE SECTION.
003700
003800 01  SW-GOOD-RECORD                      PIC X VALUE 'Y'.
003900
004000 01  FILE-AT-END          PIC X VALUE 'N'.
004100*
005800 01  COUNTERS-AND-ACCUMULATORS.
005900     05  CTR-REJECT-RECORDS              PIC  S9(5)
006000         PACKED-DECIMAL         VALUE 0.
006100     05  CTR-RECORDS-READ                PIC  S9(5)
006200         PACKED-DECIMAL         VALUE 0.
006300     05  CTR-RECORDS-WRITTEN             PIC  S9(5)
006400         PACKED-DECIMAL         VALUE 0.
006500
006600 PROCEDURE DIVISION.
006700     PERFORM INITIALIZATION
006800     PERFORM PROCESS-ALL
006900        UNTIL FILE-AT-END = 'Y'
007000     PERFORM TERMINATION
007100     GOBACK.
007200
007300 INITIALIZATION.
007400     OPEN INPUT INPUT-FILE
007500          OUTPUT GOOD-FILE
007600     PERFORM READ-PAR.
007700
007800 PROCESS-ALL.
007900     MOVE 'Y' TO SW-GOOD-RECORD
008000     PERFORM SELECT-THE-RECORD
008100     IF SW-GOOD-RECORD  = 'Y'
008200     THEN
008300*      THE RECORD IS GOOD, I.E. TO BE SELECTED
008400       PERFORM WRITE-GOOD-RECORD
008500       ADD 1 TO CTR-RECORDS-WRITTEN
008600     ELSE
008700*      THE RECORD IS  NOT GOOD, NOT WRITTEN OUT, SKIPPED
008800       ADD 1 TO CTR-REJECT-RECORDS
008900     END-IF
009000
009100     PERFORM READ-PAR.
009200
009300 WRITE-GOOD-RECORD.
009400     WRITE GOOD-RECORD FROM EMPLOYEE-RECORD.
009500
009600 TERMINATION.
009700*    Suppose no good records were written out
009800*    that would mean either
009900*        your selection criteria were not right
010000*        you have the wrong input file
010100*        it so happens there are no chosen records in input file
010200*    in any case, you want to know about the situation
010300     IF CTR-RECORDS-WRITTEN = 0
010400     THEN
010500         GO TO ERROR-EXIT
010600     END-IF
010700
010800     CLOSE INPUT-FILE
010900          GOOD-FILE.
011000
```

5. SELECT1. The Record Selection Program.

```
011100 SELECT-THE-RECORD.
011200*     the value 02000 is hard coded for this example
011300     IF  ER-EMPLOYEE-NUMBER  > '02000'
011400     THEN CONTINUE
011500     ELSE
011600         MOVE 'N' TO SW-GOOD-RECORD
011700     END-IF.
011800
011900 READ-PAR.
012000     READ INPUT-FILE
012100         AT END MOVE 'Y' TO FILE-AT-END
012200     NOT AT END
012300         ADD 1 TO CTR-RECORDS-READ
012400     END-READ.
012500
012600 ERROR-EXIT.
012700     DISPLAY 'THERE WERE NO RECORDS WRITTEN TO THE OUTPUT FILE'
012800     DISPLAY 'PROGRAM ABORTED'
012900     CLOSE INPUT-FILE
013000          GOOD-FILE.
013100     GOBACK.
```

The input data file **EMP**: (the next two lines are a column ruler)

```
         1         2         3         4         5         6
123456789.123456789.123456789.123456789.123456789.123456789.12345678

      01000  PEARLE E GATES             D0001 01
      02000  LED BALOON                 D0002 04
      03000  ORTIZ, DAVID               D0005 06
      04000  JOE JONES                  D0504 01
```

Here is sample JCL:

```
//STEP1      EXEC PGM=SELECT1
//STEPLIB DD DSN=your.executable.program.library.here,DISP=SHR
//*  THE NEXT LIBRARY NAME MAY BE DIFFERENT AT YOUR CO
//EMP       DD   DSN=userid.COBBOOK.DATA(EMP),DISP=SHR
//GOODFI    DD   SYSOUT=*
//SYSOUT    DD   SYSOUT=*
//SYSUDUMP  DD   SYSOUT=*
```

Expected results:

```
      01000  PEARLE E GATES          D0001 01
      02000  LED BALOON              D0002 04
      03000  ORTIZ, DAVID            D0005 06
      04000  JOE JONES               D0504 01
```

6. VALID1. The Edit or Validate Program

VALID1.

Similar to The Record Selection Program, #5 above, but produces a report. It typically writes out the "good" records to a file, as in The Sequence Check Program, #4, but it also prints out the "bad" records on a report. If some were invalid, it prints out or displays a noticeable error message.

Please compare this program to the Selection program and to the Sequence Check program. The logic is very similar. The Edit or Validate program will check every record of the input file against certain criteria. These criteria might be:

    all number fields contain valid numerics

    all data fields contain data - not spaces

    certain fields contain data that is found on a table (see the programs EVAL1, DIRSUB1, SERSRCH1, BINSRCH1.

6. VALID1. The Edit or Validate Program

The program **VALID1:**

```
000200 IDENTIFICATION DIVISION.
000300* Validate input data
000400*  if good, write to output file
000500*  if bad, print out on report
000600 PROGRAM-ID. VALID1.
000700 ENVIRONMENT DIVISION.
000800 INPUT-OUTPUT SECTION.
000900 FILE-CONTROL.
001000*      INPUT FILE EMP1
001100      SELECT INPUT-FILE ASSIGN EMP1.
001500*      OUTPUT FILE VALIDFI SEND TO PRINTER
001510      SELECT VALID-FILE ASSIGN VALIDFI.
001900*      REPORTFI SEND TO PRINTER
002000      SELECT REPORT-FILE ASSIGN REPORTFI.
002300
002400 DATA DIVISION.
002500 FILE SECTION.
002600
002700 FD   INPUT-FILE
002800      RECORDING MODE IS F
003100      RECORD CONTAINS 80 CHARACTERS.
003200 01   INPUT-RECORD.
003210      05   FILLER                     PIC X(8).
003220      05   FILLER                     PIC X(01).
003230      05   ER-EMPLOYEE-NUMBER         PIC X(05).
003240      05   FILLER                     PIC X(01).
003250      05   ER-EMPLOYEE-NAME           PIC X(25).
003260      05   FILLER                     PIC X(01).
003270      05   ER-EMPLOYEE-DEPARTMENT     PIC X(05).
003280      05   FILLER                     PIC X(01).
003290      05   ER-EMPLOYEE-SALARY-CODE    PIC X(02).
003300      05   FILLER                     PIC X(01).
003310      05   FILLER                     PIC X(30).
003320
003400 FD   VALID-FILE
003500      RECORDING MODE IS F
003800      RECORD CONTAINS 80 CHARACTERS.
003900 01   VALID-RECORD                    PIC X(80).
004000
```

6. VALID1. The Edit or Validate Program

```
004100 FD   REPORT-FILE
004200      RECORDING MODE IS F
004500      RECORD CONTAINS 133 CHARACTERS.
004700
004800 01  REPORT-REC                    PIC X(133).
004900
005000 WORKING-STORAGE SECTION.
005100
005200 01  SW-VALID-RECORD               PIC X VALUE 'Y'.
005300
005400 01  FILE-AT-END                   PIC X VALUE 'N'.
005500*
007200 01  COUNTERS-AND-ACCUMULATORS.
007300     05  CTR-INVALID-RECORDS          PIC  S9(5)
007400           PACKED-DECIMAL        VALUE 0.
007500     05  CTR-RECORDS-READ             PIC  S9(5)
007600           PACKED-DECIMAL        VALUE 0.
007700     05  CTR-RECORDS-WRITTEN          PIC  S9(5)
007800           PACKED-DECIMAL        VALUE 0.
007900
008000 01  TITLE-HEADING-LINE.
008100     05  FILLER                    PIC X(1) VALUE SPACES.
008200     05  FILLER                    PIC X(35)
008300           VALUE 'VALIDATION PROGRAM'.
008400     05  FILLER                    PIC X(04) VALUE SPACES.
008500     05  FILLER                    PIC X(33)
008600           VALUE 'INVALID RECORDS         '.
008700     05  REPORT-DATE.
008800         10  REPORT-YY  PIC 99.
008900         10  REPORT-MM  PIC 99.
009000         10  REPORT-DD  PIC 99.
009100     05  FILLER                    PIC X(29) VALUE SPACES.
009200     05  PAGE-LIT-FLD              PIC X(5)  VALUE 'PAGE '.
009300     05  PAGE-NUMBER               PIC 9(2)  VALUE 1.
009400
009500 01  DETAIL-INVALID-LINE.
009600     05  FILLER                    PIC X(1)  VALUE SPACES.
009700     05  REASON-INVALID            PIC X(30) VALUE SPACES.
009800     05  RECORD-IMAGE              PIC X(80) VALUE SPACES.
009900
010000 PROCEDURE DIVISION.
010200     PERFORM INITIALIZATION
010300     PERFORM PROCESS-ALL
010400        UNTIL FILE-AT-END = 'Y'
010500     PERFORM TERMINATION
010600     GOBACK.
010700
010800 INITIALIZATION.
010900     OPEN INPUT INPUT-FILE
011000          OUTPUT VALID-FILE
011100                 REPORT-FILE
011200     PERFORM READ-PAR
011300     ACCEPT REPORT-DATE FROM DATE.
011400
```

6. VALID1. The Edit or Validate Program

```
011500 PROCESS-ALL.
011600     MOVE SPACES TO DETAIL-INVALID-LINE
011700     MOVE 'Y' TO SW-VALID-RECORD
011800     PERFORM VALIDATE-THE-RECORD
011900     IF SW-VALID-RECORD  = 'Y'
012000     THEN
012100        PERFORM WRITE-VALID-RECORD
012200        ADD 1 TO CTR-RECORDS-WRITTEN
012300     ELSE
012400        PERFORM PRINT-INVALID-LINE
012500        ADD 1 TO CTR-INVALID-RECORDS
012600     END-IF
012700
012800     PERFORM READ-PAR.
012900
013000 WRITE-VALID-RECORD.
013100     WRITE VALID-RECORD FROM INPUT-RECORD.
013200
013300 PRINT-INVALID-LINE.
013400     MOVE INPUT-RECORD TO RECORD-IMAGE IN DETAIL-INVALID-LINE
013500     WRITE REPORT-REC FROM DETAIL-INVALID-LINE.
013600
013700 TERMINATION.
013800     IF CTR-RECORDS-WRITTEN = 0
013900     THEN
014000        GO TO ERROR-EXIT
014100     END-IF
014200
014300     CLOSE INPUT-FILE
014400           VALID-FILE
014500           REPORT-FILE.
014600
```

6. VALID1. The Edit or Validate Program

```
014700 VALIDATE-THE-RECORD.
014800*    If there is anything wrong with the record,
014900*    move 'N' to sw-valid-record.
015000     IF  ER-EMPLOYEE-NUMBER       IS NUMERIC
015100     THEN CONTINUE
015200     ELSE
015300         MOVE 'EMPLOYEE NUM NOT NUMERIC' TO REASON-INVALID
015400         MOVE 'N' TO SW-VALID-RECORD
015500     END-IF
015600     IF  ER-EMPLOYEE-NUMBER          = SPACES
015700     THEN
015800         MOVE 'BAD EMPLOYEE NUMBER    ' TO REASON-INVALID
015900         MOVE 'N' TO SW-VALID-RECORD
016000     END-IF
016100     IF  ER-EMPLOYEE-NAME            = SPACES
016200     THEN
016300         MOVE 'BAD EMPLOYEE NAME      ' TO REASON-INVALID
016400         MOVE 'N' TO SW-VALID-RECORD
016500     END-IF
016600     IF  ER-EMPLOYEE-DEPARTMENT      = SPACES
016700     THEN
016800         MOVE 'BAD EMPLOYEE DEPARTMENT' TO REASON-INVALID
016900         MOVE 'N' TO SW-VALID-RECORD
017000     END-IF
017100     IF  ER-EMPLOYEE-SALARY-CODE     = SPACES
017200     THEN
017300         MOVE 'BAD EMPLOYEE SALARY CODE' TO REASON-INVALID
017400         MOVE 'N' TO SW-VALID-RECORD
017500     END-IF.
017600*    Other things you might check are:
017700*      numeric fields numeric?
017800*      numbers within range
017900*      code is found within a table (table lookup/search verb)
018000*      check whether all fields filled in, etc
018100*    if a field fails the test, move 'n' to valid-flag
018200*    if a field passes the test, do nothing
018300*    complex conditions are best expressed with positives, not ne
018400*    example: if input-code is equal to '1' or '2' or '3'
018500*    then continue
018600*    else
018700*    move 'N' to valid-flag
018800*    end-if.
018900
019000 READ-PAR.
019100     READ INPUT-FILE
019200         AT END MOVE 'Y' TO FILE-AT-END
019300     NOT AT END
019400       ADD 1 TO CTR-RECORDS-READ
019500     END-READ.
019600
019700 ERROR-EXIT.
019800     DISPLAY 'THERE WERE' CTR-RECORDS-WRITTEN 'GOOD RECORDS'
019900     DISPLAY 'THERE WERE' CTR-INVALID-RECORDS 'INVALID RECORDS'
020000     DISPLAY 'PROGRAM ABORTED'
020100*     AT YOUR COMPANY YOU MIGHT CALL AN ABEND ROUTINE HERE
020200     CLOSE INPUT-FILE
020300           VALID-FILE
020400           REPORT-FILE.
020500     GOBACK.
```

37

6. VALID1. The Edit or Validate Program

The input data file **EMP1**: (the next two lines are a column ruler)

```
         1         2         3         4         5         6
123456789.123456789.123456789.123456789.123456789.123456789.12345678

        00001 ZONE, CAL                D0001 01
        00002 RAMIREZ, MANNY           D0004 02
        00003 PEDD, MOE                D0003 04
        00004 MANDER, SAL A.           D0029 09
        00005 BEARER, PAUL             D0003 03
        00006 AARON, HANK              D0003 01
        00025 COBB, TY                 D0022 24
        00032 BONDS, BARRY             D0008 23
        00041 YONARA, CY               D0004 22
        00051 DEAN, JAMES              D0002 13
        00054 GATOR, AL E.             D0005 07
        00056 TYME, JUSTIN             D0004 08
        00057 CASE, JUSTIN             D0004 03
        01000 PEARLE E GATES           D0001 01
        03000 ORTIZ, DAVID             D0005 06
        02000 LED BALOON               D0002 04
        04000 JOE JONES                D0504 01
```

Here is sample JCL:

```
//STEP1      EXEC PGM=VALID1
//STEPLIB DD DSN=your.executable.program.library.here,DISP=SHR
//*   THE NEXT LIBRARY NAME MAY BE DIFFERENT AT YOUR CO
//EMP1        DD    DSN=userid.COBBOOK.DATA(EMP1),DISP=SHR
//VALIDFI     DD    SYSOUT=*
//REPORTFI    DD    SYSOUT=*
//SYSOUT      DD    SYSOUT=*
//SYSUDUMP    DD    SYSOUT=*
```

Expected output:

```
        00001 ZONE, CAL                D0001 01
        00002 RAMIREZ, MANNY           D0004 02
        00003 PEDD, MOE                D0003 04
        00004 MANDER, SAL A.           D0029 09
        00005 BEARER, PAUL             D0003 03
        00006 AARON, HANK              D0003 01
        00025 COBB, TY                 D0022 24
        00032 BONDS, BARRY             D0008 23
        00041 YONARA, CY               D0004 22
        00051 DEAN, JAMES              D0002 13
        00054 GATOR, AL E.             D0005 07
        00056 TYME, JUSTIN             D0004 08
        00057 CASE, JUSTIN             D0004 03
        01000 PEARLE E GATES           D0001 01
```

7. BRKLV1. The One Level Subtotal (Control Break) Program

BRKLV1.
Similar to The Simple, Single File Report Program with record count or final totals, #3 above, but with a big difference: it checks for a "break" (the control break) in some field, such as account number, and when the break occurs prints out subtotals for the amounts pertaining to the field. At end of the file, it prints out totals of the amounts (grand or final totals).

Now we are getting into the Real World! One large, all-inclusive grand total may not be detailed enough. Each department of the company may want to see *just its totals:* enter the program that shows subtotals by department. Each department head can inspect just the part of the report that interests her or him, while the chief financial officer will flip through the report to the last page to devour the grand all-inclusive totals, and know whether to declare bankruptcy or not.

7. BRKLV1. The One Level Subtotal (Control Break) Program

```
000200  IDENTIFICATION DIVISION.
000300* 1 level control break - on state
000400* this is an excellent example of a 1 level control break
000500* (subtotal) program.  Use it as a model.
000600 PROGRAM-ID. BRKLV1.
000700 ENVIRONMENT DIVISION.
000800 CONFIGURATION SECTION.
000900 INPUT-OUTPUT SECTION.
001000 FILE-CONTROL.
001100*    INPUT FILE IS SALES1
001200     SELECT SALES-FILE  ASSIGN SALES1.
001500*  OUTPUT FILE IS SENT TO THE PRINTER
001600     SELECT REPORT-FILE  ASSIGN REPORTFI.
001900
002000 DATA DIVISION.
002100 FILE SECTION.
002200*
002300 FD  SALES-FILE
002400     RECORDING MODE IS F
002700     RECORD CONTAINS  80 CHARACTERS.
002800*
002900 01  SALES-RECORD.
003000*    Program assumes that input data is sorted by state
003100*    state is the field that the program "breaks" on
003200     05  SR-STATE            PIC X(02).
003300     05  FILLER              PIC X(03).
003400     05  SR-BRANCH           PIC X(10).
003500     05  SR-SALESPERSON      PIC X(15).
003600     05  FILLER              PIC X(05).
003700     05  SR-ITEM-SOLD        PIC X(15).
003800     05  FILLER              PIC X(05).
003900     05  SR-AMOUNT-SOLD      PIC S9(7)V99.
004000     05  FILLER              PIC X(16).
004100*
004200 FD  REPORT-FILE
004300     RECORDING MODE IS F
004600     RECORD CONTAINS 133 CHARACTERS.
004700*
004800 01  REPORT-RECORD           PIC X(133).
004900*
```

7. BRKLV1. The One Level Subtotal (Control Break) Program

```
005000 WORKING-STORAGE SECTION.
005100 01   SWITCHES.
005200     05   FILE-AT-END            PIC X   VALUE 'N'.
005300*
005400 01   ACCUMULATORS.
005500     05   GRAND-TOTAL-ACCUM PIC S9(9)V99 PACKED-DECIMAL VALUE +0.
005600     05   STATE-ACCUM       PIC S9(9)V99 PACKED-DECIMAL VALUE +0.
005700*
005800 01   LINE-AND-PAGE-CTRS.
005900     05   LINE-CTR              PIC S9(3)
006000              PACKED-DECIMAL VALUE +0.
006100     05   MAX-LINES-PER-PAGE   PIC S9(3)
006200              PACKED-DECIMAL VALUE +40.
006300     05   PAGE-CTR             PIC S9(3)
006400          PACKED-DECIMAL VALUE +0.
006500*
006600 01   SAVE-AREAS.
006700*    AN AREA TO HOLD THE FIELD THAT THE PROGRAM 'BREAKS' ON
006800*    IT MUST HAVE SAME PICTURE AS THE ITEM IT HOLDS
006900     05   SAVE-STATE           PIC X(02) VALUE SPACES.
007000*
007100 01   PRINT-LINES.
007200     05   GRAND-TOTAL-LINE.
007300        10   FILLER            PIC X(02) VALUE SPACES.
007400        10   FILLER            PIC X(20)
007500             VALUE '*** GRAND TOTAL ***'.
007600        10   FILLER            PIC X(43) VALUE SPACES.
007700        10   GTL-AMOUNT-SOLD   PIC  Z(9).99-.
007800*
007900     05   STATE-TOTAL-LINE.
008000        10   FILLER            PIC X(08) VALUE SPACES.
008100        10   FILLER            PIC X(20)
008200             VALUE '*** TOTAL FOR ***'.
008300        10   STL-STATE         PIC X(02) VALUE SPACES.
008400        10   FILLER            PIC X(22) VALUE SPACES.
008500        10   STL-AMOUNT-SOLD   PIC  Z(9).99-.
008600**
008700     05   DETAIL-PRINT-LINE.
008800        10   FILLER            PIC X(05) VALUE SPACES.
008900        10   DPL-STATE         PIC X(02) VALUE SPACES.
009000        10   FILLER            PIC X(05) VALUE SPACES.
009100        10   DPL-BRANCH        PIC X(10) VALUE SPACES.
009200        10   FILLER            PIC X(06) VALUE SPACES.
009300        10   DPL-SALESPERSON   PIC X(15) VALUE SPACES.
009400        10   FILLER            PIC X(05) VALUE SPACES.
009500        10   DPL-ITEM-SOLD     PIC X(15) VALUE SPACES.
009600        10   FILLER            PIC X(04) VALUE SPACES.
009700        10   DPL-AMOUNT-SOLD   PIC  Z(7).99-.
009800**
009900 01   BLANK-LINE.
010000     05   FILLER               PIC X(133) VALUE SPACES.
010100**
```

7. BRKLV1. The One Level Subtotal (Control Break) Program

```
010200 01   HEADING-LINE-1.
010300      05  FILLER                  PIC X(30) VALUE SPACES.
010400      05  FILLER                  PIC X(40)
010500      VALUE 'MODEL CONTROL BREAK REPORT'.
010600      05  FILLER                  PIC X(50) VALUE SPACES.
010700      05  HL1-PAGE                PIC ZZZ.
010800**
010900 01   HEADING-LINE-2.
011000      05  FILLER                  PIC X(2) VALUE SPACES.
011100      05  FILLER                  PIC X(10)
011200          VALUE 'STATE'.
011300      05  FILLER                  PIC X(16)
011400          VALUE 'BRANCH'.
011500      05  FILLER                  PIC X(20)
011600          VALUE 'SALESPERSON'.
011700**
011800 PROCEDURE DIVISION.
011900      PERFORM INITIALIZATION
012000      PERFORM PRODUCE-THE-REPORT
012100          UNTIL FILE-AT-END = 'Y'
012200      PERFORM TERMINATION
012300      GOBACK.
012400**
012500 INITIALIZATION.
012600      OPEN INPUT SALES-FILE
012700      OPEN OUTPUT REPORT-FILE
012800      PERFORM READ-A-RECORD
012900**    SAVE CONTROL FIELD
013000      MOVE SR-STATE         TO SAVE-STATE
013100      MOVE ZEROS TO GTL-AMOUNT-SOLD
013200      MOVE ZEROS TO STL-AMOUNT-SOLD
013300      MOVE ZEROS TO DPL-AMOUNT-SOLD
013400      PERFORM PRINT-HEADER-LINES.
013500**
013600 PRODUCE-THE-REPORT.
013700**
013800      PERFORM DETAIL-PROCESSING
013900      PERFORM READ-A-RECORD.
014000
```

7. BRKLV1. The One Level Subtotal (Control Break) Program

```
014100 DETAIL-PROCESSING.
014200**    IF THERE IS A CHANGE IN THE CONTROL FIELD,
014300**        PERFORM THE CONTROL BREAK ROUTINE
014400       IF SR-STATE          IS NOT EQUAL TO SAVE-STATE
014500       THEN PERFORM STATE-BREAK
014600       END-IF
014700**    THE FOLLOWING IS DETAIL PROCESSING
014800**    ADD INPUT AMOUNT TO FIRST LEVEL ACCUMULATOR
014900**    COUNT INPUT RECORDS
015000**    PRINT A DETAIL LINE
015100**    ADD DETAIL AMOUNT    TO LOWEST LEVEL (STATE) TOTAL.
015200       ADD SR-AMOUNT-SOLD  TO STATE-ACCUM
015300**    FORMAT DETAIL LINE FOR PRINTING.
015400**    PRINT  DETAIL LINE.
015500       MOVE SR-STATE        TO DPL-STATE
015600       MOVE SR-BRANCH       TO DPL-BRANCH
015700       MOVE SR-SALESPERSON  TO DPL-SALESPERSON
015800       MOVE SR-ITEM-SOLD    TO DPL-ITEM-SOLD
015900       MOVE SR-AMOUNT-SOLD  TO DPL-AMOUNT-SOLD
016000       WRITE REPORT-RECORD FROM DETAIL-PRINT-LINE
016100           AFTER ADVANCING 1 LINE
016200       ADD 1 TO LINE-CTR
016300       IF LINE-CTR  IS GREATER THAN MAX-LINES-PER-PAGE
016400       THEN PERFORM PRINT-HEADER-LINES
016500       END-IF.
016600**
```

7. BRKLV1. The One Level Subtotal (Control Break) Program

```
016700 STATE-BREAK.
016800**    WRITE OUT THIS LEVEL TOTALS (STATE)
016900**    ADD THIS LEVEL TOTAL (STATE) TO GRAND TOTAL
017000**    ZERO OUT THIS LEVEL TOTALS (STATE)
017100**    SAVE THIS LEVEL INPUT CONTROL FIELD (SAVE INPUT STATE)
017200**
017300       PERFORM PRINT-STATE-TOTALS
017600       ADD STATE-ACCUM TO GRAND-TOTAL-ACCUM
017610       MOVE ZERO TO STATE-ACCUM
017620       MOVE SR-STATE TO SAVE-STATE.
017700**
017800 PRINT-STATE-TOTALS.
017900       MOVE SAVE-STATE TO STL-STATE
018000       MOVE STATE-ACCUM TO STL-AMOUNT-SOLD
018100       WRITE REPORT-RECORD FROM STATE-TOTAL-LINE
018200            AFTER ADVANCING 3 LINES
018300       WRITE REPORT-RECORD FROM BLANK-LINE
018400       AFTER ADVANCING 2 LINES
018500       ADD 5 TO LINE-CTR
018600       IF LINE-CTR    IS GREATER THAN MAX-LINES-PER-PAGE
018700       THEN PERFORM PRINT-HEADER-LINES
018800       END-IF.
018900**
019000 PRINT-GRAND-TOTALS.
019100       MOVE GRAND-TOTAL-ACCUM TO GTL-AMOUNT-SOLD
019200       WRITE REPORT-RECORD FROM GRAND-TOTAL-LINE
019300            AFTER ADVANCING 3 LINES.
019400* *
019500 PRINT-HEADER-LINES.
019600       ADD  1 TO PAGE-CTR
019700       MOVE PAGE-CTR TO HL1-PAGE
019800       MOVE 0 TO LINE-CTR
019900       WRITE REPORT-RECORD FROM HEADING-LINE-1
020000            AFTER ADVANCING PAGE
020100       WRITE REPORT-RECORD FROM HEADING-LINE-2
020200            AFTER ADVANCING 1 LINE
020300       WRITE REPORT-RECORD FROM BLANK-LINE
020400            AFTER ADVANCING 3 LINES.
020500**
020600 READ-A-RECORD.
020700       READ SALES-FILE
020800       AT END MOVE  'Y' TO FILE-AT-END
021000       END-READ.
021100
022000 TERMINATION.
022100**   HAVE TO PERFORM THE BREAK, BECAUSE END OF FILE IS LIKE A BREAK
022200       PERFORM STATE-BREAK
022300**   PRINT FINAL TOTALS, DISPLAY RECORD COUNTS, IF ANY
022400       PERFORM PRINT-GRAND-TOTALS
022500       CLOSE SALES-FILE
022600            REPORT-FILE.
```

7. BRKLV1. The One Level Subtotal (Control Break) Program

The input data file **SALES1**: (the next two lines are a column ruler)

```
         1         2         3         4         5         6
123456789.123456789.123456789.123456789.123456789.123456789.12345678

CT   HARTFORD   ANN SAMUELS      CHEVELLE       000800000
CT   HARTFORD   THIERRY HENRI    FERRARI        006000000
CT   NEW HAVEN  ANNA JONES       OMNI           000030000
CT   NEW HAVEN  ANNA JONES       STING RAY      000200000
CT   NEW HAVEN  ANNA JONES       STING RAY      000200000
CT   NEW HAVEN  ANNA JONES       STING RAY      000200000
CT   NEW HAVEN  JETER, DEREK     CAMARO         000600000
CT   NEW HAVEN  CAL ZONI         JAGUAR         009000000
CT   NEW HAVEN  CAL ZONI         PEUGEOT        000200000
CT   NEW HAVEN  ROSE BUSH        PINTO          000040000
MA   BOSTON     JOE JONES        HONDA          000010000
MA   BOSTON     RON ZONEY        LEMON          000020000
MA   BOSTON     RON ZONEY        SUBARU         000010000
MI   DETROIT    CAM NEWTON       EDSEL          000000010
MI   DETROIT    CAM NEWTON       FIAT           004000000
MI   DETROIT    CAM NEWTON       FORD           000020000
MI   DETROIT    CAM NEWTON       STUDEBAKER     000000600
NY   ALBANY     JERRY RICE       CONTINENTAL    002000000
NY   ALBANY     JERRY RICE       ESCORT         000010000
NY   ALBANY     JERRY RICE       FORD           000010000
NY   ALBANY     JERRY RICE       HYUNDAI        000010000
NY   ALBANY     JERRY RICE       HYUNDAI        000010000
NY   ROCHESTER  BILL E. GOAT     MASERATI       000001000
```

Here is sample JCL:

```
//STEP1     EXEC PGM=BRKLV1
//STEPLIB DD DSN=your.executable.program.library.here,DISP=SHR
//*   THE NEXT LIBRARY NAME MAY BE DIFFERENT AT YOUR CO
//SALES1    DD   DSN=userid.COBBOOK.DATA(SALES1),DISP=SHR
//REPORTFI  DD   SYSOUT=*
//SYSOUT    DD   SYSOUT=*
//SYSUDUMP  DD   SYSOUT=*
```

7. BRKLV1. The One Level Subtotal (Control Break) Program

Expected output:

```
                         MODEL CONTROL BREAK REPORT
STATE       BRANCH       SALESPERSON

   CT       HARTFORD     ANN SAMUELS      CHEVELLE        8000.00
   CT       HARTFORD     THIERRY HENRI    FERRARI        60000.00
   CT       NEW HAVEN    ANNA JONES       OMNI             300.00
   CT       NEW HAVEN    ANNA JONES       STING RAY       2000.00
   CT       NEW HAVEN    ANNA JONES       STING RAY       2000.00
   CT       NEW HAVEN    ANNA JONES       STING RAY       2000.00
   CT       NEW HAVEN    JETER, DEREK     CAMARO          6000.00
   CT       NEW HAVEN    CAL ZONI         JAGUAR         90000.00
   CT       NEW HAVEN    CAL ZONI         PEUGEOT         2000.00
   CT       NEW HAVEN    ROSE BUSH        PINTO            400.00
      ***  TOTAL FOR  ***    CT               172700.00

   MA       BOSTON       JOE JONES        HONDA            100.00
   MA       BOSTON       RON ZONEY        LEMON            200.00
   MA       BOSTON       RON ZONEY        SUBARU           100.00
      ***  TOTAL FOR  ***    MA                  400.00

   MI       DETROIT      CAM NEWTON       EDSEL               .10
   MI       DETROIT      CAM NEWTON       FIAT           40000.00
   MI       DETROIT      CAM NEWTON       FORD             200.00
   MI       DETROIT      CAM NEWTON       STUDEBAKER         6.00
      ***  TOTAL FOR  ***    MI                40206.10

   NY       ALBANY       JERRY RICE       CONTINENTAL    20000.00
   NY       ALBANY       JERRY RICE       ESCORT           100.00
   NY       ALBANY       JERRY RICE       FORD             100.00
   NY       ALBANY       JERRY RICE       HYUNDAI          100.00
   NY       ALBANY       JERRY RICE       HYUNDAI          100.00
   NY       ROCHESTER    BILL E. GOAT     MASERATI          10.00
      ***  TOTAL FOR  ***    NY                20410.00

                         MODEL CONTROL BREAK REPORT
STATE       BRANCH       SALESPERSON

***  GRAND TOTAL  ***                                   233716.10
```

8. BRKLV3. The Three Level Subtotal (Control Break) Program

BRKLV3.

Similar to the One Level Subtotal (Control Break) Program, #7 above, but now there are three levels of subtotals, corresponding to three levels of fields in the data. Typical levels might be Salesperson within State within District. If you can handle this program, you can handle a Two or Four or Six or Eleven level program.

This program is even more Real World. Most businesses are organized in a hierarchical manner - Salesperson within Department within District within Region is typical. Each level of the company has its director. She or he will want to know everything about her or his level and everything under it. This report provides everything needed for those long meetings and discussions about "how we did last quarter."

8. BRKLV3. The Three Level Subtotal (Control Break) Program

The program **BRKLV3:**

```
000200 IDENTIFICATION DIVISION.
000300* 3 level control break - model program
000400* this is an excellent example of a 3 level control break
000500* (subtotal) program.  Use it as a model.
000600 PROGRAM-ID. BRKLV3.
000700 ENVIRONMENT DIVISION.
000800 CONFIGURATION SECTION.
000900 INPUT-OUTPUT SECTION.
001000 FILE-CONTROL.
001100     SELECT SALES-FILE ASSIGN SALES3.
001400     SELECT REPORT-FILE ASSIGN REPORTFI.
001700*
001800 DATA DIVISION.
001900 FILE SECTION.
002000*
002100 FD  SALES-FILE
002200     RECORDING MODE IS F
002400     RECORD CONTAINS  80 CHARACTERS.
002600*
002700 01  SALES-RECORD.
002800*      The program assumes that the input data is sorted
002900*         by salesperson within branch within state
003000     05  SR-STATE          PIC X(02).
003100     05  FILLER            PIC X(03).
003200     05  SR-BRANCH         PIC X(10).
003400     05  SR-SALESPERSON    PIC X(15).
003500     05  FILLER            PIC X(05).
003600     05  SR-ITEM-SOLD      PIC X(15).
003700     05  FILLER            PIC X(05).
003800     05  SR-AMOUNT-SOLD    PIC S9(7)V99.
003900     05  FILLER            PIC X(16).
004000*
004100 FD  REPORT-FILE
004200     RECORDING MODE IS F
004400     RECORD CONTAINS 133 CHARACTERS.
004600*
004700 01  REPORT-RECORD          PIC X(133).
004800*
```

8. BRKLV3. The Three Level Subtotal (Control Break) Program

```
004900 WORKING-STORAGE SECTION.
005000 01   SWITCHES.
005100      05   FILE-AT-END               PIC X   VALUE 'N'.
005200*
005300 01   ACCUMULATORS.
005400      05   GRAND-TOTAL-ACCUM         PIC S9(9)V99
005500           PACKED-DECIMAL VALUE +0.
005600      05   STATE-ACCUM               PIC S9(9)V99
005700           PACKED-DECIMAL VALUE +0.
005800      05   BRANCH-ACCUM              PIC S9(9)V99
005900           PACKED-DECIMAL VALUE +0.
006000      05   SALESPERSON-ACCUM         PIC S9(9)V99
006100           PACKED-DECIMAL VALUE +0.
006200*
006300 01   LINE-AND-PAGE-CTRS.
006400      05   LINE-CTR                  PIC S9(3)
006500           PACKED-DECIMAL VALUE +0.
006600      05   MAX-LINES-PER-PAGE        PIC S9(3)
006700           PACKED-DECIMAL VALUE +40.
006800      05   PAGE-CTR                  PIC S9(3)
006900           PACKED-DECIMAL VALUE +0.
007000*      *
007100 01   SAVE-AREAS.
007200      05   SAVE-STATE                PIC X(02) VALUE SPACES.
007300      05   SAVE-BRANCH               PIC X(10) VALUE SPACES.
007400      05   SAVE-SALESPERSON          PIC X(15) VALUE SPACES.
007500*
007600 01   PRINT-LINES.
007700      05   GRAND-TOTAL-LINE.
007800           10   FILLER               PIC X(02) VALUE SPACES.
007900           10   FILLER               PIC X(20)
008000                VALUE '*** GRAND TOTAL ***'.
008100           10   FILLER               PIC X(43) VALUE SPACES.
008200           10   GTL-AMOUNT-SOLD      PIC Z(9).99-.
008300*
008400      05   STATE-TOTAL-LINE.
008500           10   FILLER               PIC X(04) VALUE SPACES.
008600           10   FILLER               PIC X(20)
008700                VALUE '***  TOTAL FOR  ***'.
008800           10   FILLER               PIC X(02) VALUE SPACES.
008900           10   STL-STATE            PIC X(02) VALUE SPACES.
009000           10   FILLER               PIC X(37) VALUE SPACES.
009100           10   STL-AMOUNT-SOLD      PIC  Z(9).99-.
009200*
009300      05   BRANCH-TOTAL-LINE.
009400           10   FILLER               PIC X(06) VALUE SPACES.
009500           10   FILLER               PIC X(20)
009600                VALUE '***  TOTAL FOR  ***'.
009700           10   FILLER               PIC X(02) VALUE SPACES.
009800           10   BTL-BRANCH           PIC X(10) VALUE SPACES.
009900           10   FILLER               PIC X(27) VALUE SPACES.
010000           10   BTL-AMOUNT-SOLD      PIC  Z(9).99-.
010100*
```

8. BRKLV3. The Three Level Subtotal (Control Break) Program

```
010200        05   SALESPERSON-TOTAL-LINE.
010300             10   FILLER                PIC X(08) VALUE SPACES.
010400             10   FILLER                PIC X(20)
010500                  VALUE '*** TOTAL FOR ***'.
010600             10   SLSTL-SALESPERSON     PIC X(15) VALUE SPACES.
010700             10   FILLER                PIC X(22) VALUE SPACES.
010800             10   SLSTL-AMOUNT-SOLD      PIC  Z(9).99-.
010900*
011000        05   DETAIL-PRINT-LINE.
011100             10   FILLER                PIC X(05) VALUE SPACES.
011200             10   DPL-STATE             PIC X(02) VALUE SPACES.
011300             10   FILLER                PIC X(05) VALUE SPACES.
011400             10   DPL-BRANCH            PIC X(10) VALUE SPACES.
011500             10   FILLER                PIC X(06) VALUE SPACES.
011600             10   DPL-SALESPERSON       PIC X(15) VALUE SPACES.
011700             10   FILLER                PIC X(05) VALUE SPACES.
011800             10   DPL-ITEM-SOLD         PIC X(15) VALUE SPACES.
011900             10   FILLER                PIC X(04) VALUE SPACES.
012000             10   DPL-AMOUNT-SOLD       PIC  Z(7).99-.
012100*
012200 01    BLANK-LINE.
012300        05   FILLER                     PIC X(133) VALUE SPACES.
012400*
012500 01    HEADING-LINE-1.
012600        05   FILLER                     PIC X(30) VALUE SPACES.
012700        05   FILLER                     PIC X(40)
012800             VALUE 'MODEL CONTROL BREAK REPORT'.
012900        05   FILLER                     PIC X(50) VALUE SPACES.
013000        05   HL1-PAGE                   PIC ZZZ.
013100*
013200 01    HEADING-LINE-2.
013300        05   FILLER                     PIC X(2) VALUE SPACES.
013400        05   FILLER                     PIC X(10)
013500             VALUE 'STATE'.
013600        05   FILLER                     PIC X(16)
013700             VALUE 'BRANCH'.
013800        05   FILLER                     PIC X(20)
013900             VALUE 'SALESPERSON'.
014000*
```

8. BRKLV3. The Three Level Subtotal (Control Break) Program

```
014100 PROCEDURE DIVISION.
014200     PERFORM INITIALIZATION
014300     PERFORM PRODUCE-THE-REPORT
014400        UNTIL FILE-AT-END = 'Y'
014500     PERFORM TERMINATION
014600     GOBACK.
014700*
014800 INITIALIZATION.
014900     OPEN INPUT SALES-FILE
015000              OUTPUT REPORT-FILE
015100     PERFORM READ-A-RECORD
015200     MOVE SR-STATE        TO SAVE-STATE
015300     MOVE SR-BRANCH       TO SAVE-BRANCH
015400     MOVE SR-SALESPERSON TO SAVE-SALESPERSON
015500     MOVE ZEROS TO GTL-AMOUNT-SOLD
015600     MOVE ZEROS TO STL-AMOUNT-SOLD
015700     MOVE ZEROS TO BTL-AMOUNT-SOLD
015800     MOVE ZEROS TO SLSTL-AMOUNT-SOLD
015900     MOVE ZEROS TO DPL-AMOUNT-SOLD
016000     PERFORM PRINT-HEADER-LINES.
016100*
016200 PRODUCE-THE-REPORT.
016300     IF SR-STATE IS NOT EQUAL TO SAVE-STATE
016400     THEN PERFORM STATE-BREAK
016500     END-IF
016600*
016700     IF SR-BRANCH IS NOT EQUAL TO SAVE-BRANCH
016800     THEN PERFORM BRANCH-BREAK
016900     END-IF
017000*
017100     IF SR-SALESPERSON IS NOT EQUAL TO SAVE-SALESPERSON
017200     THEN PERFORM SALESPERSON-BREAK
017300     END-IF
017400*
017500     PERFORM DETAIL-PROCESSING
017600     PERFORM READ-A-RECORD.
017700
017800 DETAIL-PROCESSING.
017900*    Add detail amount   to lowest level (salesperson) total.
018000*    format detail line for printing.
018100*    print  detail line.
018200     ADD SR-AMOUNT-SOLD  TO SALESPERSON-ACCUM
018300     MOVE SR-STATE        TO DPL-STATE
018400     MOVE SR-BRANCH       TO DPL-BRANCH
018500     MOVE SR-SALESPERSON TO DPL-SALESPERSON
018600     MOVE SR-ITEM-SOLD    TO DPL-ITEM-SOLD
018700     MOVE SR-AMOUNT-SOLD TO DPL-AMOUNT-SOLD
018800     WRITE REPORT-RECORD FROM DETAIL-PRINT-LINE
018900        AFTER ADVANCING 1 LINE
019000     ADD 1 TO LINE-CTR
019100     IF LINE-CTR  IS GREATER THAN MAX-LINES-PER-PAGE
019200     THEN PERFORM PRINT-HEADER-LINES
019300     END-IF.
019400*
```

8. BRKLV3. The Three Level Subtotal (Control Break) Program

```
019500 STATE-BREAK.
019600*    Highest level break.
019700*    perform next lower level break (branch)
019800*    write out this level (state) totals
019900*    add this level totals (state) to next level (grand total)
020000*    zero out this level totals (state)
020100*    save this level input field (save input state)
020200*  if program requirements dictate, perform print-header-lines.
020300*
020400     PERFORM BRANCH-BREAK
020450
020500     PERFORM PRINT-STATE-TOTALS
020600     ADD STATE-ACCUM TO GRAND-TOTAL-ACCUM
020700     MOVE ZERO TO STATE-ACCUM
020800     MOVE SR-STATE TO SAVE-STATE.
020900*
021000 BRANCH-BREAK.
021100*    Middle level break
021200*    perform next level break (salesperson)
021300*    write out this level totals (branch)
021400*    add this level totals (branch) to next level (state)
021500*    zero out this level totals (branch)
021600*    save this level input field (save input branch)
021700*
021800     PERFORM SALESPERSON-BREAK
021900     PERFORM PRINT-BRANCH-TOTALS
022000     ADD BRANCH-ACCUM TO STATE-ACCUM
022100     MOVE ZERO TO BRANCH-ACCUM
022200     MOVE SR-BRANCH TO SAVE-BRANCH.
022300*
022400 SALESPERSON-BREAK.
022500*    Lowest level break
022600*    write out this level totals (salesperson)
022700*    add this level total (salesperson) to next level (branch)
022800*    zero out this level totals (salesperson)
022900*    save this level input field (save input salesperson)
023000*
023100     PERFORM PRINT-SALESPERSON-TOTALS
023200     ADD SALESPERSON-ACCUM TO BRANCH-ACCUM
023300     MOVE ZERO TO SALESPERSON-ACCUM
023400     MOVE SR-SALESPERSON TO SAVE-SALESPERSON.
023500*
```

8. BRKLV3. The Three Level Subtotal (Control Break) Program

```
023600 PRINT-STATE-TOTALS.
023700      MOVE SAVE-STATE TO STL-STATE
023800      MOVE STATE-ACCUM TO STL-AMOUNT-SOLD
023900      WRITE REPORT-RECORD FROM STATE-TOTAL-LINE
024000         AFTER ADVANCING 3 LINES
024100      WRITE REPORT-RECORD FROM BLANK-LINE
024200         AFTER ADVANCING 2 LINES
024300      ADD 5 TO LINE-CTR
024400      IF LINE-CTR     IS GREATER THAN MAX-LINES-PER-PAGE
024500      THEN PERFORM PRINT-HEADER-LINES
024600      END-IF.
024700*
024800 PRINT-BRANCH-TOTALS.
024900      MOVE SAVE-BRANCH TO BTL-BRANCH
025000      MOVE BRANCH-ACCUM TO BTL-AMOUNT-SOLD
025100      WRITE REPORT-RECORD FROM BRANCH-TOTAL-LINE
025200         AFTER ADVANCING 3 LINES
025300      WRITE REPORT-RECORD FROM BLANK-LINE
025400         AFTER ADVANCING 2 LINES
025500      ADD 5 TO LINE-CTR
025600      IF LINE-CTR     IS GREATER THAN MAX-LINES-PER-PAGE
025700      THEN PERFORM PRINT-HEADER-LINES
025800      END-IF.
025900*
026000 PRINT-SALESPERSON-TOTALS.
026100      MOVE SAVE-SALESPERSON TO SLSTL-SALESPERSON
026200      MOVE SALESPERSON-ACCUM TO SLSTL-AMOUNT-SOLD
026300      WRITE REPORT-RECORD FROM SALESPERSON-TOTAL-LINE
026400         AFTER ADVANCING 3 LINES
026500      WRITE REPORT-RECORD FROM BLANK-LINE
026600         AFTER ADVANCING 2 LINES
026700      ADD 5 TO LINE-CTR
026800      IF LINE-CTR     IS GREATER THAN MAX-LINES-PER-PAGE
026900      THEN PERFORM PRINT-HEADER-LINES
027000      END-IF.
027100*
027200 PRINT-GRAND-TOTALS.
027300      MOVE GRAND-TOTAL-ACCUM TO GTL-AMOUNT-SOLD
027400      WRITE REPORT-RECORD FROM GRAND-TOTAL-LINE
027500         AFTER ADVANCING 3 LINES.
027600*
```

8. BRKLV3. The Three Level Subtotal (Control Break) Program

```
027700 PRINT-HEADER-LINES.
027800     ADD  1 TO PAGE-CTR
027900     MOVE PAGE-CTR TO HL1-PAGE
028000     MOVE 0 TO LINE-CTR
028100     WRITE REPORT-RECORD FROM HEADING-LINE-1
028200        AFTER ADVANCING PAGE
028300     WRITE REPORT-RECORD FROM HEADING-LINE-2
028400        AFTER ADVANCING 1 LINE
028500     WRITE REPORT-RECORD FROM BLANK-LINE
028600        AFTER ADVANCING 3 LINES.
028800 READ-A-RECORD.
028900     READ SALES-FILE
029000        AT END MOVE 'Y' TO FILE-AT-END
029200     END-READ.
030200 TERMINATION.
030300     PERFORM STATE-BREAK
030400     PERFORM PRINT-GRAND-TOTALS
030500     CLOSE SALES-FILE
030600           REPORT-FILE.
```

The input data file **SALES3**: (the next two lines are a column ruler)

```
         1         2         3         4         5         6
123456789.123456789.123456789.123456789.123456789.123456789.12345678
CT    HARTFORD   ANN SAMUELS      CHEVELLE          000800000
CT    HARTFORD   THIERRY HENRI    FERRARI           006000000
CT    NEW HAVEN  ANNA JONES       OMNI              000030000
CT    NEW HAVEN  ANNA JONES       STING RAY         000200000
CT    NEW HAVEN  ANNA JONES       STING RAY         000200000
CT    NEW HAVEN  ANNA JONES       STING RAY         000200000
CT    NEW HAVEN  JETER, DEREK     CAMARO            000600000
CT    NEW HAVEN  CAL ZONI         JAGUAR            009000000
CT    NEW HAVEN  CAL ZONI         PEUGEOT           000200000
CT    NEW HAVEN  ROSE BUSH        PINTO             000040000
MA    BOSTON     JOE JONES        HONDA             000010000
MA    BOSTON     RON ZONEY        LEMON             000020000
MA    BOSTON     RON ZONEY        SUBARU            000010000
MI    DETROIT    CAM NEWTON       EDSEL             000000010
MI    DETROIT    CAM NEWTON       FIAT              004000000
MI    DETROIT    CAM NEWTON       FORD              000020000
MI    DETROIT    CAM NEWTON       STUDEBAKER        000000600
NY    ALBANY     JERRY RICE       CONTINENTAL       002000000
NY    ALBANY     JERRY RICE       ESCORT            000010000
NY    ALBANY     JERRY RICE       FORD              000010000
NY    ALBANY     JERRY RICE       HYUNDAI           000010000
NY    ALBANY     JERRY RICE       HYUNDAI           000010000
NY    ROCHESTER  BILL E. GOAT     MASERATI          000001000
```

Here is sample JCL:

```
//STEP1     EXEC PGM=BRKLV3
//STEPLIB DD DSN=your.executable.program.library.goes.here,DISP=SHR
//*  THE NEXT LIBRARY NAME MAY BE DIFFERENT AT YOUR COMPANY
//SALES3    DD    DSN=userid.COBBOOK.DATA(SALES3),DISP=SHR
//REPORTFI  DD    SYSOUT=*
//SYSOUT    DD    SYSOUT=*
//SYSUDUMP  DD    SYSOUT=*
```

8. BRKLV3. The Three Level Subtotal (Control Break) Program

Expected output:

```
1                               MODEL CONTROL BREAK REPORT
    STATE       BRANCH          SALESPERSON
-
    CT      HARTFORD        ANN SAMUELS           CHEVELLE            8000.00
-       *** TOTAL FOR ***   ANN SAMUELS                               8000.00
0
    CT      HARTFORD        THIERRY HENRI         FERRARI            60000.00
-       *** TOTAL FOR ***   THIERRY HENRI                            60000.00
0
-    ***   TOTAL FOR   ***   HARTFORD                                68000.00
0
    CT      NEW HAVEN       ANNA JONES            OMNI                 300.00
    CT      NEW HAVEN       ANNA JONES            STING RAY           2000.00
    CT      NEW HAVEN       ANNA JONES            STING RAY           2000.00
    CT      NEW HAVEN       ANNA JONES            STING RAY           2000.00
-       *** TOTAL FOR ***   ANNA JONES                                6300.00
0
    CT      NEW HAVEN       JETER, DEREK          CAMARO              6000.00
-       *** TOTAL FOR ***   JETER, DEREK                              6000.00
0
    CT      NEW HAVEN       CAL ZONI              JAGUAR             90000.00
    CT      NEW HAVEN       CAL ZONI              PEUGEOT             2000.00
-       *** TOTAL FOR ***   CAL ZONI                                 92000.00
0
    CT      NEW HAVEN       ROSE BUSH             PINTO                400.00
-       *** TOTAL FOR ***   ROSE BUSH                                  400.00
0
0
1                               MODEL CONTROL BREAK REPORT
    STATE       BRANCH          SALESPERSON
-
-    ***   TOTAL FOR   ***   NEW HAVEN                              104700.00
0
-   ***   TOTAL FOR   ***   CT                                     172700.00
0
    MA      BOSTON          JOE JONES             HONDA                100.00
-       *** TOTAL FOR ***   JOE JONES                                  100.00
0
    MA      BOSTON          RON ZONEY             LEMON                200.00
    MA      BOSTON          RON ZONEY             SUBARU               100.00
-       *** TOTAL FOR ***   RON ZONEY                                  300.00
0
-       *** TOTAL FOR ***   RON ZONEY                                  300.00
0
-    ***   TOTAL FOR   ***   BOSTON                                   400.00
0
-   ***   TOTAL FOR   ***   MA                                        400.00
```

(Continues on next page)

8. BRKLV3. The Three Level Subtotal (Control Break) Program

```
0
      MI      DETROIT       CAM NEWTON      EDSEL                          .10
      MI      DETROIT       CAM NEWTON      FIAT                     40000.00
      MI      DETROIT       CAM NEWTON      FORD                       200.00
      MI      DETROIT       CAM NEWTON      STUDEBAKER                   6.00
-         *** TOTAL FOR ***   CAM NEWTON                             40206.10
0
1                                MODEL CONTROL BREAK REPORT
   STATE      BRANCH         SALESPERSON
-
-      ***  TOTAL FOR  ***   DETROIT                                 40206.10
0
-    ***  TOTAL FOR  ***    MI                                       40206.10
0
      NY      ALBANY        JERRY RICE      CONTINENTAL              20000.00
      NY      ALBANY        JERRY RICE      ESCORT                     100.00
      NY      ALBANY        JERRY RICE      FORD                       100.00
      NY      ALBANY        JERRY RICE      HYUNDAI                    100.00
      NY      ALBANY        JERRY RICE      HYUNDAI                    100.00
-         *** TOTAL FOR ***   JERRY RICE                            20400.00
0
-      ***  TOTAL FOR  ***   ALBANY                                  20400.00
0
      NY      ROCHESTER     BILL E. GOAT    MASERATI                    10.00
-         *** TOTAL FOR ***   BILL E. GOAT                            10.00
0
0
-      ***  TOTAL FOR  ***   ROCHESTER                                10.00
0
-    ***  TOTAL FOR  ***    NY                                       20410.00
0
1                                MODEL CONTROL BREAK REPORT
   STATE      BRANCH         SALESPERSON
-
-  *** GRAND TOTAL ***                                             233716.10
```

9. FILEUPD1. The Sequential File, Batch Update Program

FILEUPD1.

It reads two files, a Master File and a Transaction File. It matches records by comparing a significant field, such as account number. A code on the Transaction Record tells it whether to Add, Change or Delete Master File records. An output file is produced that contains the added, changed and unchanged Master File records.

Credit card file maintenance: approved customers now can carry plastic money as they are added to the huge cardholder file (Add transactions.) Some souls will have their wallets/pocketbooks lightened a bit, since they are being dropped from the file and have to turn in their credit cards (Delete transactions.) Those who have kept within their credit limit and have paid on time will see their credit limit raised to 3 times the size of the national debt of Mauritania! (Change transactions.)

It's one program that processes Adds, Deletes and Changes. It is usually done in Batch mode (not done on a terminal while someone waits, and waits....) Batch mode in the IBM mainframe world means that the job was submitted through JCL and runs when it runs. The results will be ready by morning (unless the programmer forgot something critical in the program...)

Most batch file update programs are designed to use transaction codes on the transaction file. If a transaction file does not come with transaction codes, I consider that to be a design flaw, because it eliminates the logic checking that is possible with transaction codes: "If this is a match, what am I doing with an Add transaction?"

All batch file update programs of this type assume that both the transaction file and the old, input master file are sorted in the same manner, on the same field or fields. If the files are not sorted this way, the program *won't work!*

The program reads the two input files: the transaction file and the old master file. It compares the key fields (sometimes called control fields) of the two files. The comparison can come out one of three ways:

The transaction key *equals* the master key.
In this case the program will *apply* the transaction to the master. This may be a change transaction or a delete transaction. It may not be an add transaction.

The transaction key is *greater than* the master key.
The program will *write out* the master record - there are no more transactions that apply to this master record.

The transaction key is *less than* the master key.
The transaction record did not find a corresponding master record. This should happen with an add transaction.

9. FILEUPD1. The Sequential File, Batch Update Program

The model program is a real Marvel. It can handle multiple transactions for the same key. It can even handle an Add, followed by a Change, then a Delete all for the same key. This will work only if the transaction file is sorted by the key, and within the key, sorted by the transaction code. Luckily Add sorts before Change which sorts before Delete.

I give you this model program for many reasons. First, because it works. This is not a trivial thing! This type of program can be a real bear. It can consume many hours of programming time before it does everything correctly. Second, because it is easier to rip code out of this program than to put it in. If you have a transaction file without Delete transactions, tear out the code for deleting. (If I were you, I'd leave it in, but commented out. Users can change their minds...) Third, because you don't *have* to rip things out if you don't need them. They will simply sit there in the program and never do anything. For example, if you *never* have multiple transactions for the same key, the program will still work perfectly, although there will be parts of the program that acquire cobwebs.

9. FILEUPD1. The Sequential File, Batch Update Program

The program **FILEUPD1:**

```
000200 IDENTIFICATION DIVISION.
000300* File update. Works fine.
000400* this is a good way to do it.  Use this as a model.
000500* transaction codes used.  Multiple trans allowed for same account
000600 PROGRAM-ID. FILEUPD1.
000700 ENVIRONMENT DIVISION.
000800 CONFIGURATION SECTION.
000900 INPUT-OUTPUT SECTION.
001000 FILE-CONTROL.
001100     SELECT TRANS-FILE  ASSIGN TRANSFIL.
001500     SELECT OLD-MASTER  ASSIGN OLDMAST.
001900     SELECT NEW-MASTER  ASSIGN NEWMAST.
002400 DATA DIVISION.
002500 FILE SECTION.
002600*
002700 FD   TRANS-FILE
002800      RECORDING MODE IS F
003100      RECORD CONTAINS  80 CHARACTERS.
003200 01   TRANS-RECORD.
003300      05   TR-ACCT-NO        PIC X(5).
003400      05   FILLER            PIC X(5).
003500      05   TR-AMOUNT         PIC 9(5).
003600      05   FILLER            PIC X(5).
003700      05   TR-CUST-NAME      PIC X(10).
003800      05   TR-TRANS-CODE     PIC X(1).
003900           88   ADD-TRANS    VALUE 'A'.
004000           88   CHANGE-TRANS VALUE 'C'.
004100           88   DELETE-TRANS VALUE 'D'.
004200      05   FILLER            PIC X(44).
004300*
004400 FD   OLD-MASTER
004500      RECORDING MODE IS F
004800      RECORD CONTAINS  80 CHARACTERS.
004900*
005000 01   OLD-MASTER-RECORD.
005100      05   OM-ACCT-NO        PIC X(05).
005200      05   FILLER            PIC X(05).
005300      05   OM-AMOUNT         PIC 9(05).
005400      05   FILLER            PIC X(05).
005500      05   OM-CUST-NAME      PIC X(10).
005600      05   FILLER            PIC X(50).
005700*
005800 FD   NEW-MASTER
005900      RECORDING MODE IS F
006200      RECORD CONTAINS  80 CHARACTERS.
006300*
006400 01   NEW-MASTER-RECORD.
006500      05   NM-ACCT-NO        PIC X(05).
006600      05   FILLER            PIC X(05).
006700      05   NM-AMOUNT         PIC 9(05).
006800      05   FILLER            PIC X(05).
006900      05   NM-CUST-NAME      PIC X(10).
007000      05   FILLER            PIC X(50).
007100*
```

9. FILEUPD1. The Sequential File, Batch Update Program

```
007200 WORKING-STORAGE SECTION.
007300 01  SWITCHES.
007400     05  MASTER-EOF                  PIC X  VALUE 'N'.
007700*
007800     05  TRANS-EOF                   PIC X  VALUE 'N'.
008100*
008200     05  SW-FINISHED-WITH-DATA       PIC X  VALUE 'N'.
008300         88  FINISHED-WITH-DATA             VALUE 'Y'.
008400         88  NOT-FINISHED-WITH-DATA         VALUE 'N'.
008500*
008600     05  SW-FIRST-TIME               PIC X  VALUE 'Y'.
008700         88  IT-IS-FIRST-TIME               VALUE 'Y'.
008800*
008900     05  SW-VALID-DELETE             PIC X  VALUE 'N'.
009000         88  VALID-DELETE                   VALUE 'Y'.
009100*
009200     05  SW-VALID-ADD               PIC X VALUE 'N'.
009300         88  VALID-ADD                      VALUE 'Y'.
009400*
009500 01  NEW-MASTER-WORK-AREA.
009600     05  WORK-NM-ACCT-NO     PIC X(05).
009700     05  FILLER              PIC X(05).
009800     05  WORK-NM-AMOUNT      PIC 9(05).
009900     05  FILLER              PIC X(05).
010000     05  WORK-NM-CUST-NAME   PIC X(10).
010100     05  FILLER              PIC X(50).
010200*
010300 PROCEDURE DIVISION.
010400*
010500     PERFORM INITIALIZATION
010600     PERFORM PROCESS-BOTH-FILES
010700        UNTIL MASTER-EOF = 'Y'
010800        AND   TRANS-EOF  = 'Y'
010900     IF FINISHED-WITH-DATA
011000     THEN
011100        PERFORM WRITE-NEW-MASTER
011200     END-IF
011300     PERFORM TERMINATION
011400     GOBACK.
011500*
011600 INITIALIZATION.
011700     OPEN INPUT TRANS-FILE
011800                OLD-MASTER
011900     OPEN OUTPUT NEW-MASTER
012000     MOVE SPACES TO NEW-MASTER-WORK-AREA
012100     MOVE 'N' TO  MASTER-EOF
012200     MOVE 'N' TO TRANS-EOF
012300     MOVE 'N' TO SW-FINISHED-WITH-DATA
012400     MOVE 'Y' TO SW-FIRST-TIME
012500     MOVE 'N'  TO SW-VALID-DELETE
012600     MOVE 'N' TO SW-VALID-ADD
012700     PERFORM GET-NEW-MASTER-DATA.
012800*
012900 PROCESS-BOTH-FILES.
013000     PERFORM WRITE-NEW-MASTER
013100     PERFORM GET-NEW-MASTER-DATA.
013200*
```

```
013300 WRITE-NEW-MASTER.
013400*     MOVE FIELDS OF WORK AREA MASTER TO NEW MASTER RECORD
013500     MOVE SPACES           TO NEW-MASTER-RECORD
013600     MOVE WORK-NM-ACCT-NO  TO NM-ACCT-NO
013700     MOVE WORK-NM-AMOUNT   TO NM-AMOUNT
013800     WRITE NEW-MASTER-RECORD.
013900*
014000 GET-NEW-MASTER-DATA.
014100     MOVE 'N' TO SW-FINISHED-WITH-DATA
014200     IF IT-IS-FIRST-TIME
014300     THEN
014400        PERFORM READ-TRANS
014500        PERFORM READ-MASTER
014600        MOVE 'N' TO SW-FIRST-TIME
014700      END-IF
014800     PERFORM COMPARE-ACCT-NO
014900        UNTIL FINISHED-WITH-DATA
015000        OR    (MASTER-EOF = 'Y'
015100              AND TRANS-EOF = 'Y').
015200*
015300 COMPARE-ACCT-NO.
015400     MOVE 'N'  TO SW-VALID-DELETE
015500     MOVE 'N'  TO SW-VALID-ADD
015600     IF MASTER-EOF IS NOT EQUAL TO 'Y'
015700     AND TRANS-EOF IS NOT EQUAL TO 'Y'
015800     THEN
015900        PERFORM MORE-RECORDS-IN-BOTH
016000     ELSE
016100        PERFORM ONE-FILE-IS-AT-END
016200     END-IF.
016300*
016400 MORE-RECORDS-IN-BOTH.
016500     IF TR-ACCT-NO IS EQUAL TO  OM-ACCT-NO
016600     THEN
016700        PERFORM TR-EQUAL-OM
016800     ELSE
016900     IF TR-ACCT-NO IS GREATER THAN OM-ACCT-NO
017000     THEN
017100        PERFORM TR-GREATER-THAN-OM
017200     ELSE
017300     IF TR-ACCT-NO IS LESS THAN OM-ACCT-NO
017400     THEN
017500        PERFORM TR-LESS-THAN-OM
017600     END-IF.
017700*
```

```
017800 ONE-FILE-IS-AT-END.
017900     IF MASTER-EOF IS EQUAL TO 'Y'
018000     THEN
018100        PERFORM ADD-THIS-TRANS-IF-POSSIBLE
018200        IF VALID-ADD
018300        THEN
018400           MOVE 'Y' TO SW-FINISHED-WITH-DATA
018500           PERFORM READ-TRANS
018600        ELSE
018700           PERFORM READ-TRANS
018800        END-IF
018900     ELSE
019000*        THERE ARE MORE MSTR RECORDS
019100        PERFORM JUST-MOVE-OM-TO-WORK
019200        MOVE 'Y' TO SW-FINISHED-WITH-DATA
019300        PERFORM READ-MASTER
019400     END-IF.
019500*
019600 TR-EQUAL-OM.
019700     PERFORM APPLY-TRANSACTION
019800     IF VALID-DELETE
019900     THEN
020000        PERFORM READ-MASTER
020100        PERFORM READ-TRANS
020200     ELSE
020300        PERFORM READ-TRANS
020400     END-IF.
020500*
020600 APPLY-TRANSACTION.
020700     IF CHANGE-TRANS
020800     THEN
020900        PERFORM PROCESS-CHANGE-TRANS
021000     ELSE
021100     IF DELETE-TRANS
021200     THEN
021300        MOVE 'Y' TO SW-VALID-DELETE
021400     ELSE
021500     IF ADD-TRANS
021600     THEN
021700        DISPLAY 'ALREADY ON FILE, CANNOT ADD THIS TRANSACTION'
021710        DISPLAY TRANS-RECORD
021720        DISPLAY SPACES
021800     END-IF.
021900*
```

9. FILEUPD1. The Sequential File, Batch Update Program

```
022000 TR-LESS-THAN-OM.
022100     PERFORM ADD-THIS-TRANS-IF-POSSIBLE
022200     IF VALID-ADD
022300     THEN
022400        MOVE 'Y' TO SW-FINISHED-WITH-DATA
022500        PERFORM READ-TRANS
022600     ELSE
022700        PERFORM READ-TRANS
022800     END-IF.
022900*
023000 ADD-THIS-TRANS-IF-POSSIBLE.
023100     IF ADD-TRANS
023200     THEN
023300        MOVE TR-ACCT-NO    TO WORK-NM-ACCT-NO
023400        MOVE TR-AMOUNT     TO WORK-NM-AMOUNT
023500        MOVE TR-CUST-NAME TO WORK-NM-CUST-NAME
023600        MOVE 'Y'    TO SW-VALID-ADD
023700     ELSE
023800        DISPLAY 'NO MATCH, CANNOT CHANGE/DELETE'
023810        DISPLAY TRANS-RECORD
023820        DISPLAY SPACES
023900     END-IF.
024000*
024100 TR-GREATER-THAN-OM.
024200     PERFORM JUST-MOVE-OM-TO-WORK
024300     MOVE 'Y' TO SW-FINISHED-WITH-DATA
024400     PERFORM READ-MASTER.
024500*
024600 JUST-MOVE-OM-TO-WORK.
024700     MOVE OM-ACCT-NO    TO WORK-NM-ACCT-NO
024800     MOVE OM-AMOUNT     TO WORK-NM-AMOUNT
024900     MOVE OM-CUST-NAME TO WORK-NM-CUST-NAME.
025000*
```

9. FILEUPD1. The Sequential File, Batch Update Program

```
025100 PROCESS-CHANGE-TRANS.
025200     IF TR-CUST-NAME IS NOT EQUAL TO SPACES
025300     THEN
025400         MOVE TR-CUST-NAME TO OM-CUST-NAME
025500     END-IF
025600     ADD TR-AMOUNT TO OM-AMOUNT.
025700 READ-MASTER.
025800     READ OLD-MASTER
025900         AT END MOVE 'Y' TO MASTER-EOF
026000     END-READ.
026200 READ-TRANS.
026300     READ TRANS-FILE
026400         AT END MOVE 'Y' TO TRANS-EOF
026500     END-READ.
026700 TERMINATION.
026800     CLOSE TRANS-FILE
026900           OLD-MASTER
027000           NEW-MASTER.
```

The input transaction data file **TRANSFIL**: (the next two lines are a column ruler)

```
         1         2         3         4         5         6
123456789.123456789.123456789.123456789.123456789.123456789.12345678

ACCT0     00100      GRUMPY     CHANGE      TRANSFIL
ACCT1     00100      SNEAZZY    ADD         TRANSFIL
ACCT1     00100      RUDOLPH    CHANGE      TRANSFIL
ACCT1     00100                 DELETE      TRANSFIL
ACCT2     00100      BLITZEN    CHANGE      TRANSFIL
ACCT4     00100      THUMPER    ADD         TRANSFIL
ACCT5     00100                 DELETE      TRANSFIL
ACCT7     00100      MR ED      ADD         TRANSFIL
ACCT8     00100      DONNER     CHANGE      TRANSFIL
ACCT8     00100      WIMPY      CHANGE      TRANSFIL
ACCT9     00100      TOTO       CHANGE      TRANSFIL
```

The old master data file **OLDMAST**: (the next two lines are a column ruler)

```
         1         2         3         4         5         6
123456789.123456789.123456789.123456789.123456789.123456789.12345678

ACCT0     00010      LOU        OLDMAST
ACCT1     00010      MOE        OLDMAST
ACCT2     00010      CURLY      OLDMAST
ACCT3     00010      HAPPY      OLDMAST
ACCT5     00010      LAUREL     OLDMAST
ACCT6     00010      HARDY      OLDMAST
ACCT8     00010      DUMBO      OLDMAST
ACCT9     00010      GEORGE     OLDMAST
```

9. FILEUPD1. The Sequential File, Batch Update Program

Here is sample JCL:
```
//STEP1     EXEC PGM=FILEUPD1
//STEPLIB DD DSN=your.executable.program.library..here,DISP=SHR
//*   THE NEXT LIBRARY NAME MAY BE DIFFERENT AT YOUR CO
//TRANSFIL  DD   DSN=userid.COBBOOK.DATA(TRANSFIL),DISP=SHR
//OLDMAST   DD   DSN=userid.COBBOOK.DATA(OLDMAST),DISP=SHR
//NEWMAST   DD   SYSOUT=*
//SYSOUT    DD   SYSOUT=*
//SYSUDUMP  DD   SYSOUT=*
```

Expected output:
```
ACCT0      00110
ACCT2      00110
ACCT3      00010
ACCT4      00100
ACCT6      00010
ACCT7      00100
ACCT8      00210
ACCT9      00110
ALREADY ON FILE, CANNOT ADD THIS TRANSACTION
ACCT1      00100      SNEAZZY    ADD         TRANSFIL
```

9. FILEUPD1. The Sequential File, Batch Update Program

This page intentionally left blank

10. SORTEX1. The COBOL Sort

SORTEX1.

This does what is known as an internal sort, I.E., the COBOL program does the sorting. The program reads an input file; while holding it in memory it sorts the records. Then it writes out the sorted records to a new output file. The suggested logic avoids misunderstandings engendered by the use of sections. It is compatible with the latest version of COBOL. (An older version of COBOL, VS COBOL worked as well, but generated disturbing error messages.) This program uses input and output procedures in which you control the logic flow and can perform input validation and output processing.

There are many ways to sort files. Some applications use a JCL Utility Sort. There are advantages to each. I show you here how to do it in COBOL. COBOL and the Utility work together in this one. You write statements in COBOL; COBOL then prepares statements in the way that the Utility wants to see them and passes them to the Utility. It does all the dirty work. You just write COBOL statements in English.

I purposely avoid the debate on which way is better: JCL Utility or COBOL statements. I don't think it's a question of what's better, but what suits your purpose better. The COBOL sort lets you do anything you want to the unsorted records before sorting them: you can select the ones you want to sort, you can rearrange fields on the record, you can drop fields or add fields. You can do whatever you want to each sorted record as soon as it gets sorted, you can produce a report, do subtotals or use the sorted file as a transaction file in a file update program.

10. SORTEX1. The COBOL Sort

The program **SORTEX1:**

```
000100 IDENTIFICATION DIVISION.
000200* Cobol sort.
000300* does not use sections; does not use go to
000400* uses sort procedures
000500* does a sort with some minimal input validation
000600* since everything is done in an orderly way,
000700* you can easily add code of your own to this program
000800 PROGRAM-ID. SORTEX1.
000900 ENVIRONMENT DIVISION.
001000 CONFIGURATION SECTION.
001100 INPUT-OUTPUT SECTION.
001200 FILE-CONTROL.
001300*     INPUT FILE UNSORTED
001400     SELECT UNSORTED-FILE ASSIGN UNSORTED.
001500*     The work file for the sort utility
001600*     you need the select and an sd but do not need jcl for it
001700     SELECT SORT-WORK      ASSIGN      SORTWORK.
001800*     output file normally a disk/tape file
001900*     for this program, send it to the printer
002000     SELECT SORTED-FILE ASSIGN SORTED.
002100*
002200 DATA DIVISION.
002300 FILE SECTION.
002400*
```

10. SORTEX1. The COBOL Sort

```
002500 FD   UNSORTED-FILE
002600      RECORDING MODE IS F
002900      RECORD CONTAINS  80 CHARACTERS.
003000
003100 01  UNSORTED-RECORD.
003200      05  WS-UR-ACCT-NO        PIC X(5).
003300      05  FILLER               PIC X(5).
003400      05  WS-UR-AMOUNT         PIC 9(5).
003500      05  WS-UR-CUST-NAME      PIC X(10).
003600      05  FILLER               PIC X(5).
003700      05  WS-UR-TRANS-CODE     PIC X(1).
003800      05  FILLER               PIC X(49).
003900
004000  SD  SORT-WORK
004400      RECORD CONTAINS  80 CHARACTERS.
004500*
004600 01  SORT-WORK-RECORD.
004700*    You need a definition and picture for
004800*    the field that is sorted on (sort key)
004900      05  SW-ACCT-NO   PIC X(05).
005000*    YOU NEED A FILLER TO COMPLETE THE DEFINITION
005100      05  FILLER        PIC X(75).
005200*
005300 FD  SORTED-FILE
005400      RECORDING MODE IS F
005700      RECORD CONTAINS  80 CHARACTERS.
005800*
005900 01  SORTED-RECORD.
006000      05  WS-SR-ACCT-NO        PIC X(05).
006100      05  FILLER               PIC X(05).
006200      05  WS-SR-AMOUNT         PIC 9(05).
006300      05  WS-SR-CUST-NAME      PIC X(10).
006400      05  FILLER               PIC X(55).
006500
006600 WORKING-STORAGE SECTION.
006700 01  SWITCHES.
006800      05  UNSORTED-FILE-AT-END    PIC X    VALUE 'N'.
006900      05  SORT-WORK-AT-END        PIC X    VALUE 'N'.
007000      05  valid-sw                PIC X    VALUE 'N'.
007100
007200 01  COUNTERS.
007300      05 RELEASED-COUNTER PIC S9(7)
007400              PACKED-DECIMAL VALUE +0.
007500      05 REJECT-COUNTER    PIC S9(7)
007600              PACKED-DECIMAL VALUE +0.
007700
007800 PROCEDURE DIVISION.
007900      PERFORM INITIALIZATION
008000*    Compare this logic to that of the simple program
008100*    notice how the sort verb replaces the
008200*    perform main until end of file etc
008300      SORT SORT-work ASCENDING KEY SW-ACCT-NO
008400          INPUT PROCEDURE SORT-INPUT
008500          OUTPUT PROCEDURE SORT-OUTPUT
008600      PERFORM       TERMINATION
008700      GOBACK.
008800
```

10. SORTEX1. The COBOL Sort

```
008900 INITIALIZATION.
009000*    Do what you normally do in initialization
009100*    open the regular input file (not the sort work file)
009200*    and other files needed
009300*    (you could open them in the sort input procedure, too)
009400     OPEN INPUT UNSORTED-FILE
009500         output SORTED-FILE
009600*    READ THE FIRST RECORD ON THE REGULAR INPUT FILE
009700     PERFORM READ-IT.
009800*    Whatever else you do in initialization
009900*    headers, initialize counters, etc
010000
010100 TERMINATION.
010200*    Do what you normally do in termination
010300*    print out total lines
010400*    close the files you opened
010500*    display totals
010600     CLOSE UNSORTED-FILE
010700           SORTED-FILE.
010800
010900 READ-IT.
011000     READ UNSORTED-FILE
011100     AT END MOVE 'Y' TO UNSORTED-FILE-AT-END
011200     END-READ.
011300
011400 SORT-INPUT.
011500*    This is the 'sort input procedure'
011600*    when control passes thru the last statement in it
011700*    the input phase of the sort is finished
011800*    and actual sorting takes place
011900     PERFORM SORT-INPUT-PROCESS-ALL
012000         UNTIL UNSORTED-FILE-AT-END = 'Y'.
012100
012200  SORT-INPUT-PROCESS-ALL.
012300* This is the point when you have each unsorted input record
012400* in your hands
012500* many programs do some validation or selection here
012600* to determine which records are actually given to the sort util
012700* we will do some simple validation here
012800     MOVE 'Y' TO VALID-SW
012900     PERFORM SORT-INPUT-VALIDATE
013000     IF VALID-SW = 'Y'
013100     THEN
013200**     Give the unsorted input record to the sort utility
013300       RELEASE SORT-work-RECord FROM unsorted-RECORD
013400       ADD 1 TO RELEASED-COUNTER
013500     ELSE
013600**     Here, you have decided not to give the unsorted input
013700**     record to the sort utility
013800       ADD 1 TO REJECT-COUNTER
013900     END-IF
014000     PERFORM READ-IT.
014100
```

10. SORTEX1. The COBOL Sort

```
014200 SORT-INPUT-VALIDATE.
014300*    Check the regular input record for validity.
014400*    if it is not suitable for sorting, set the valid sw
014500*    other validation criteria would apply for other files
014600     IF WS-UR-ACCT-NO IS equal to spaces
014700        THEN MOVE 'N' TO VALID-SW
014800     END-IF.
014900
015000 SORT-OUTPUT.
015100*    This is the 'sort output procedure'
015200*    when control passes thru the last statement in it
015300*    the output phase of the sort is finished
015400*    you have seen (returned) the last sorted record
015500*    and the sort utility is finished
015600     PERFORM RETURN-IT
015700     PERFORM SORT-OUTPUT-PROCESS-ALL
015800        UNTIL SORT-WORK-AT-END = 'Y'.
015900
016000 RETURN-IT.
016100*    Gets each sorted record from the sort utility
016200*    return is logically like a read
016300      RETURN SORT-work
016400         AT END MOVE 'Y' TO SORT-work-AT-END
016500      END-RETURN.
016600
016700 SORT-OUTPUT-PROCESS-ALL.
016800      PERFORM SORT-OUTPUT-PROCESSING
016900      PERFORM RETURN-IT.
017100 SORT-OUTPUT-PROCESSING.
017200* Here you do the things you do in a
017300* regular program's main processing routine
017400* add totals, compute things
017500* write detail records, print lines, etc
017600* you could put control break check here
017700* this program just and writes the record out to "sorted file"
017900      MOVE SORT-WORK-RECORD TO SORTED-RECORD
018100      WRITE SORTED-RECORD.
```

10. SORTEX1. The COBOL Sort

The input transaction data file **UNSORTED** (the next two lines are a column ruler)

```
         1         2         3         4         5         6
123456789.123456789.123456789.123456789.123456789.123456789.12345678

ACCT0      00100      GRUMPY      CHANGE      TRANSFIL
ACCT8      00100      WIMPY       CHANGE      TRANSFIL
ACCT1      00100      SNEAZZY     ADD         TRANSFIL
ACCT1      00100      SNEAZZY     ADD         TRANSFIL
ACCT1      00100      RUDOLPH     CHANGE      TRANSFIL
ACCT1      00100                  DELETE      TRANSFIL
ACCT4      00100      THUMPER     ADD         TRANSFIL
ACCT5      00100                  DELETE      TRANSFIL
ACCT7      00100      MR ED       ADD         TRANSFIL
ACCT8      00100      DONNER      CHANGE      TRANSFIL
ACCT9      00100      TOTO        CHANGE      TRANSFIL
```

Here is sample JCL:

```
//STEP1     EXEC PGM=SORTEX1
//STEPLIB DD DSN=your.executable.program.library.goes.here,DISP=SHR
//*  THE NEXT LIBRARY NAME MAY BE DIFFERENT AT YOUR COMPANY
//*IT'S POSSIBLE THAT YOU WILL NEED MORE JCL BECAUSE OF THE SORT
//UNSORTED   DD   DSN=userid.COBBOOK.DATA(UNSORTED),DISP=SHR
//SORTED     DD   SYSOUT=*
//SYSOUT     DD   SYSOUT=*
//SYSUDUMP   DD   SYSOUT=*
```

Expected output:

```
ACCT0      00100      GRUMPY      CHANGE      TRANSFIL
ACCT1      00100      RUDOLPH     CHANGE      TRANSFIL
ACCT1      00100                  DELETE      TRANSFIL
ACCT1      00100      SNEAZZY     ADD         TRANSFIL
ACCT1      00100      SNEAZZY     ADD         TRANSFIL
ACCT4      00100      THUMPER     ADD         TRANSFIL
ACCT5      00100                  DELETE      TRANSFIL
ACCT7      00100      MR ED       ADD         TRANSFIL
ACCT8      00100      WIMPY       CHANGE      TRANSFIL
ACCT8      00100      DONNER      CHANGE      TRANSFIL
ACCT9      00100      TOTO        CHANGE      TRANSFIL
```

11. EVAL1. The CASE Structure: EVALUATE

EVAL1.

This program illustrates a possible use for EVALUATE. It reads a file containing part number but no part name. It uses EVALUATE to make the decisions that will supply the missing part name. A table lookup would be more realistic for this application, but this is here to illustrate EVALUATE, not table lookup!

I suggest looking up the section on EVALUATE in your COBOL book
The program **EVAL1:**

```
000200 IDENTIFICATION DIVISION.
000300 PROGRAM-ID. EVAL1.
000400* Read a regular file
000500* checks each record to see if it has a valid part number
000600* uses evaluate to replace blank part name with part name
000700 ENVIRONMENT DIVISION.
000800 CONFIGURATION SECTION.
000900 INPUT-OUTPUT SECTION.
001000 FILE-CONTROL.
001100* INPUT FILE PARTS1
001200     SELECT INFILE ASSIGN PARTS1.
001500 DATA DIVISION.
001600 FILE SECTION.
001700
001800 FD  INFILE
001900     RECORDING MODE IS F
002210     RECORD CONTAINS 80 CHARACTERS.
002300 01  INFILE-RECORD.
003100     05  PART-NUMBER     PIC X(6).
003200     05  PART-NAME       PIC X(30).
003300     05  QTY-ON-HAND     PIC 9(3).
003400     05  QTY-ON-ORDER    PIC 9(3).
003500     05  QTY-ON-RESERVE  PIC 9(3).
003600     05  PART-PRICE      PIC 9(3)V99.
003700     05  UNUSED          PIC X(30).
002400
002500 WORKING-STORAGE SECTION.
002600 01 SWITCHES.
002700     05  INFILE-AT-END   PIC X  VALUE 'N'.
002800     05  VALID-SW        PIC X  VALUE 'Y'.
002900
003900 PROCEDURE DIVISION.
004000     PERFORM INITIALIZATION
004100     PERFORM PROCESS-ALL
004200         UNTIL INFILE-AT-END = 'Y'
004300     PERFORM TERMINATION
004400     GOBACK.
004500
004600 INITIALIZATION.
004700     OPEN INPUT INFILE
004800     PERFORM READ-PAR.
004900
```

11. EVAL1. The CASE Structure: EVALUATE

```
005000 PROCESS-ALL.
005100     MOVE 'Y' TO VALID-SW
005200     PERFORM EVALUATE-PARTS
005300     IF VALID-SW = 'Y'
005400     THEN DISPLAY INFILE-RECORD
005500*        Not doing anything else in this program
005600*        but you could write out records,
005700*        print lines in report, etc
005800     ELSE DISPLAY 'BAD RECORD' INFILE-RECORD
005900     END-IF
006000     PERFORM READ-PAR.
006100
006200 TERMINATION.
006300     CLOSE INFILE.
006500 READ-PAR.
006600     READ INFILE
006700         AT END MOVE 'Y' TO INFILE-AT-END
006800     END-READ.
007000 EVALUATE-PARTS.
007100     EVALUATE PART-NUMBER
007200         WHEN 'PART01' MOVE 'WIDGETS'
007300           TO PART-NAME
007400         WHEN 'PART03' MOVE 'LEAD WINGED GLIDERS'
007500           TO PART-NAME
007600         WHEN 'PART04' MOVE 'LEFT FOOT REEBOCKS'
007700           TO PART-NAME
007800         WHEN 'PART06' MOVE '286 COMPUTERS W 4K HARD DISK'
007900           TO PART-NAME
008000     WHEN OTHER
008100         MOVE 'UNKNOWN' TO PART-NAME
008200         MOVE 'N' TO VALID-SW
008300     END-EVALUATE.
```

The input data file **PARTS1**: (the next two lines are a column ruler)

```
         1         2         3         4         5         6
123456789.123456789.123456789.123456789.123456789.123456789.12345678

PART01                                003 007 002 10022
PART02                                004 006 001 14054
PART04                                021 002 004 04323
PART06                                043 077 012 00042
```

Here is sample JCL:

```
//STEP1     EXEC PGM=EVAL1
//STEPLIB DD DSN=your.executable.program.library..here,DISP=SHR
//*   THE NEXT LIBRARY NAME MAY BE DIFFERENT AT YOUR CO
//PARTS1    DD   DSN=userid.COBBOOK.DATA(PARTS1),DISP=SHR
//SYSOUT    DD   SYSOUT=*
//SYSUDUMP  DD   SYSOUT=*
```

Expected output: (DISPLAYS are not formatted any particular way)

```
PART01WIDGETS                        003 007 002 10022
BAD RECORDPART02UNKNOWN                    004 006 001 14054
PART04LEFT FOOT REEBOCKS             021 002 004 04323
PART06286 COMPUTERS W 4K HARD DISK   043 077 012 00042
```

12. DIRSUB1. Direct Subscripting

DIRSUB1.

This is direct subscripting - you know the subscript, you use it to reference the desired occurrence in the table. Given an 8 on the input record, you want AUGUST.

Direct subscripting probably won't be the only thing you do in a program. It will most likely be used in a larger, more complex program, such as a report program. It will allow you to change fields on the input record, based on a table of items that are always numbered in the same way. A good example would be the months of the year: January is always 1 and December is always 12.

The program **DIRSUB1**:

```
000200 IDENTIFICATION DIVISION.
000300* DIRECT SUBSCRIPTING
000400 PROGRAM-ID. DIRSUB1.
000500*  GENERAL LOGIC FOR PROGRAM THAT READS EVERY INPUT RECORD
000600*  AFTER LOOKING UP THE EMPLOYEE'S MONTH OF HIRE ON A TABLE,
000700*     BY DIRECT SUBSCRIPTING,
000800*  IT WRITES IT OUT TO AN OUTPUT FILE
000900 ENVIRONMENT DIVISION.
001000 INPUT-OUTPUT SECTION.
001100 FILE-CONTROL.
001200*    INPUT FILE EMP2
001300     SELECT INPUT-FILE ASSIGN EMP2.
001700*    REPORTFI: A REPORT FILE, PRINTS OUT INFORMATION ON EMPLOYEES
001800*        WITH MONTH OF HIRE, SEND TO PRINTER
001900     SELECT REPORT-FILE ASSIGN REPORTFI.
002300
002400 DATA DIVISION.
002500 FILE SECTION.
002600
002700 FD  INPUT-FILE
002800     RECORDING MODE IS F
003100     RECORD CONTAINS 80 CHARACTERS.
003200 01  INPUT-RECORD.
003210*            INPUT RECORD DESCRIPTION
003230     05  FILLER                      PIC X(8).
003230     05  FILLER                      PIC X(01).
003240     05  ER-EMPLOYEE-NUMBER          PIC X(05).
003250     05  FILLER                      PIC X(01).
003260     05  ER-EMPLOYEE-NAME            PIC X(25).
003270*    05  FILLER                      PIC X(01).
003280     05  ER-EMPLOYEE-DEPARTMENT      PIC X(05).
003290     05  FILLER                      PIC X(01).
003300     05  ER-EMPLOYEE-SALARY-CODE     PIC X(02).
003310     05  FILLER                      PIC X(01).
003320*    MONTH OF HIRE MUST BE DEFINED AS NUMERIC,
003330*     TO USE DIRECT SUBSCRIPTING
003340     05  ER-MONTH-OF-HIRE            PIC 9(02).
003350     05  FILLER                      PIC X(28).
003360
```

12. DIRSUB1. Direct Subscripting

```
003400 FD   REPORT-FILE
003500      RECORDING MODE IS F
003800      RECORD CONTAINS 133 CHARACTERS.
003900
004000 01   REPORT-RECORD                     PIC X(133).
004100
004200 WORKING-STORAGE SECTION.
004300
004400 01   FILE-AT-END          PIC X VALUE 'N'.
004500*
004600 01   SW-VALID-RECORD      PIC X VALUE 'Y'.
004700
006700 01   COUNTERS-AND-ACCUMULATORS.
006800      05  CTR-RECORDS-READ             PIC  S9(5)
006900           PACKED-DECIMAL  VALUE +0.
007000      05  CTR-RECORDS-WRITTEN          PIC S9(5)
007100           PACKED-DECIMAL  VALUE +0.
007200
007300 01   TITLE-HEADING-LINE.
007400      05  FILLER                       PIC X(1) VALUE SPACES.
007500      05  FILLER                       PIC X(35)
007600             VALUE 'EMPLOYEE RECORDS WITH MONTH OF HIRE'.
007700      05  FILLER                       PIC X(04) VALUE SPACES.
007800      05  FILLER                       PIC X(33)
007900             VALUE SPACES.
008000      05  REPORT-DATE                  PIC X(8).
008100
008200 01   DETAIL-PRINT-LINE.
008300      05  FILLER                       PIC X(1) VALUE SPACES.
008400      05  DL-MONTH-OF-HIRE             PIC X(09).
008500      05  DL-RECORD-IMAGE              PIC X(80) VALUE SPACES.
008600
008700 01   MONTH-TABLE-LITERALS.
008800      05 FILLER PIC X(9) VALUE 'JANUARY'.
008900      05 FILLER PIC X(9) VALUE 'FEBRUARY'.
009000      05 FILLER PIC X(9) VALUE 'MARCH'.
009100      05 FILLER PIC X(9) VALUE 'APRIL'.
009200      05 FILLER PIC X(9) VALUE 'MAY'.
009300      05 FILLER PIC X(9) VALUE 'JUNE'.
009400      05 FILLER PIC X(9) VALUE 'JULY'.
009500      05 FILLER PIC X(9) VALUE 'AUGUST'.
009600      05 FILLER PIC X(9) VALUE 'SEPTEMBER'.
009700      05 FILLER PIC X(9) VALUE 'OCTOBER'.
009800      05 FILLER PIC X(9) VALUE 'NOVEMBER'.
009900      05 FILLER PIC X(9) VALUE 'DECEMBER'.
010000
010100 01   MONTH-TABLE REDEFINES MONTH-TABLE-LITERALS.
010200      05 EACH-MONTH PIC X(9) OCCURS 12 TIMES.
010300
```

12. DIRSUB1. Direct Subscripting

```
010400 PROCEDURE DIVISION.
010500     PERFORM INITIALIZATION
010600     PERFORM PROCESS-ALL UNTIL
010700        FILE-AT-END = 'Y'
010800     PERFORM TERMINATION
010900     GOBACK.
011000
011100 INITIALIZATION.
011200     OPEN INPUT INPUT-FILE
011300         OUTPUT REPORT-FILE
011400     WRITE REPORT-RECORD FROM TITLE-HEADING-LINE
011500     PERFORM READ-PAR
011600
011700     ACCEPT REPORT-DATE FROM DATE.
011800
011900 PROCESS-ALL.
012000     MOVE EACH-MONTH(ER-MONTH-OF-HIRE) TO DL-MONTH-OF-HIRE
012100     MOVE INPUT-RECORD TO DL-RECORD-IMAGE
012200     WRITE REPORT-RECORD FROM DETAIL-PRINT-LINE
012300
012400     PERFORM READ-PAR.
012500
012600 TERMINATION.
012700
012800     CLOSE INPUT-FILE
012900          REPORT-FILE.
013000
013100 READ-PAR.
013200     READ INPUT-FILE
013300     AT END
013400        MOVE 'Y' TO FILE-AT-END
013500     NOT AT END
013600        ADD 1 TO CTR-RECORDS-READ
013700     END-READ.
```

12. DIRSUB1. Direct Subscripting

The input data file **EMP2**: (the next two lines are a column ruler)
```
         1         2         3         4         5         6
123456789.123456789.123456789.123456789.123456789.123456789.12345678

        01000  PEARLE E GATES          D0001 01 05
        02000  LED BALOON              D0002 04 09
        03000  ORTIZ, DAVID            D0005 06 01
        04000  JOE JONES               D0504 01 12
```

Here is sample JCL:
```
//STEP1     EXEC PGM=DIRSUB1
//STEPLIB DD DSN=your.executable.program.library.here,DISP=SHR
//*  THE NEXT LIBRARY NAME MAY BE DIFFERENT AT YOUR CO
//EMP2       DD   DSN=userid.COBBOOK.DATA(EMP2),DISP=SHR
//REPORTFI   DD   SYSOUT=*
//SYSOUT     DD   SYSOUT=*
//SYSUDUMP   DD   SYSOUT=*
```

Expected output:
```
EMPLOYEE RECORDS WITH MONTH OF HIRE
MAY                01000 PEARLE E GATES          D0001 01 05
SEPTEMBER          02000 LED BALOON              D0002 04 09
JANUARY            03000 ORTIZ, DAVID            D0005 06 01
DECEMBER           04000 JOE JONES               D0504 01 12
```

13. SERSRCH1. The Sequential Search

SERSRCH1.

This is a table lookup This program checks whether data exists on a table or array contained within the program, using the SEARCH verb.

Many training coordinators tell the instructor explicitly to make sure the students can handle table lookups. The best advice I can give you is master this! Insurance companies, banks, government agencies (to mention just a few) live on table lookups.

Make sure yours are coded properly - check out values at the beginning, middle and end of the table.

The sequential, or serial search is used when the entries in the table are not in order. It is probably a good choice when there are less than 100 or so entries in the table.

Note that a COBOL table has nothing to do with a DB2 table.

13. SERSRCH1. The Sequential Search

The program **SERSRCH1:**

```
000200 IDENTIFICATION DIVISION.
000300 PROGRAM-ID. SERSRCH1.
000400* The serial search
000500* reads every input record
000600* after looking up the employee's month of hire on a table,
000700* by a sequential search, it writes it out to an output file
000800 ENVIRONMENT DIVISION.
000900 INPUT-OUTPUT SECTION.
001000 FILE-CONTROL.
001100*     INPUT FILE EMP2
001200     SELECT INPUT-FILE ASSIGN EMP2.
001600*     REPORTFI: A REPORT FILE, PRINTS OUT INFORMATION ON EMPLOYEES
001700*         WITH MONTH OF HIRE, SEND TO PRINTER
001800     SELECT REPORT-FILE ASSIGN REPORTFI.
002200
002300 DATA DIVISION.
002400 FILE SECTION.
002500
002600 FD  INPUT-FILE
002700     RECORDING MODE IS F
003000     RECORD CONTAINS 80 CHARACTERS.
003100 01  INPUT-RECORD.
003120     05  FILLER                      PIC X(08).
002130     05  FILLER                      PIC X(01).
003140     05  ER-EMPLOYEE-NUMBER          PIC X(05).
003150     05  FILLER                      PIC X(01).
003160     05  ER-EMPLOYEE-NAME            PIC X(25).
003170     05  ER-EMPLOYEE-DEPARTMENT      PIC X(05).
003180     05  FILLER                      PIC X(01).
003190     05  ER-EMPLOYEE-SALARY-CODE     PIC X(02).
003200     05  FILLER                      PIC X(01).
003210*     MONTH OF HIRE CAN BE DEFINED AS CHARACTER (ALPHANUMERIC)
003230     05  ER-MONTH-OF-HIRE            PIC X(02).
003230     05  FILLER                      PIC X(29).
003230
```

13. SERSRCH1. The Sequential Search

```
003300 FD   REPORT-FILE
003400      RECORDING MODE IS F
003700      RECORD CONTAINS 133 CHARACTERS.
003800
003900 01   REPORT-RECORD                      PIC X(133).
004000
004100 WORKING-STORAGE SECTION.
004200
004300 01   FILE-AT-END          PIC X VALUE 'N'.
004400*
004500 01   SW-VALID-RECORD      PIC X VALUE 'Y'.
004600
006400 01   COUNTERS-AND-ACCUMULATORS.
006500      05   CTR-RECORDS-READ               PIC  S9(5)
006600           PACKED-DECIMAL        VALUE 0.
006700      05   CTR-RECORDS-WRITTEN            PIC  S9(5)
006800           PACKED-DECIMAL        VALUE 0.
006900
007000 01   TITLE-HEADING-LINE.
007100      05   FILLER                         PIC X(1) VALUE SPACES.
007200      05   FILLER                         PIC X(35)
007300                 VALUE 'EMPLOYEE RECORDS WITH MONTH OF HIRE'.
007400      05   FILLER                         PIC X(04) VALUE SPACES.
007500      05   FILLER                         PIC X(33) VALUE SPACES.
007700      05   REPORT-DATE.
007800           10   REPORT-YY  PIC 99.
007900           10   REPORT-MM  PIC 99.
008000           10   REPORT-DD  PIC 99.
008100
008200 01   DETAIL-PRINT-LINE.
008300      05   FILLER                         PIC X(1) VALUE SPACES.
008400      05   DL-MONTH-OF-HIRE               PIC X(09).
008500      05   DL-RECORD-IMAGE                PIC X(80) VALUE SPACES.
008600
008700 01   MONTH-TABLE-LITERALS.
008800*    This is hard coding a COBOL table.
008900*    Examine the code to see what is happening.
009100*    these are fillers, because you
009200*    won't be referring to them directly, by name
009300*    notice how the code (01) is written right
009400*    beside the name (january)
009500*    all the pictures must be the same.
009600*    the literals inside of quotes don't have
009700*     to be the same length, but many will code them that way
009800           05      FILLER    PIC X(11)     VALUE '01JANUARY'.
009900           05      FILLER    PIC X(11)     VALUE '02FEBRUARY'.
010000           05      FILLER    PIC X(11)     VALUE '03MARCH'.
010100           05      FILLER    PIC X(11)     VALUE '04APRIL'.
010200           05      FILLER    PIC X(11)     VALUE '05MAY'.
010300           05      FILLER    PIC X(11)     VALUE '06JUNE'.
010400           05      FILLER    PIC X(11)     VALUE '07JULY'.
010500           05      FILLER    PIC X(11)     VALUE '08AUGUST'.
010600           05      FILLER    PIC X(11)     VALUE '09SEPTEMBER'.
010700           05      FILLER    PIC X(11)     VALUE '10OCTOBER'.
010800           05      FILLER    PIC X(11)     VALUE '11NOVEMBER'.
010900           05      FILLER    PIC X(11)     VALUE '12DECEMBER'.
```

13. SERSRCH1. The Sequential Search

```
011100*     Redefines means that this 01 level item
011200*     occupies the same spot in memory as the one it redefines
011300*     so actually the two 01 levels are
011400*     the same thing with different names and different picture
011500 01  MONTH-TABLE REDEFINES MONTH-TABLE-LITERALS.
011600*    Next item must occur as many times
011700*    as there are fillers in the preceding 01
011800*    its picture or the pictures under it
011900*    must add up to the same number as the
012000*    picture in the fillers above (11 in this example)
012100    05    EACH-MONTH-INFO    OCCURS 12 TIMES
012200*    You need the indexed by clause
012300*    if you're going to use the search verb
012400*    this defines and creates the index -
012500*    so no pictures for the index, please
012600             INDEXED BY MONTH-INDEX.
012700          10  EACH-MONTH-NUMBER          PIC XX.
012800          10  EACH-MONTH-NAME            PIC X(09).
012900
013000 PROCEDURE DIVISION.
013100     PERFORM INITIALIZATION
013200     PERFORM PROCESS-ALL UNTIL
013300        FILE-AT-END = 'Y'
013400     PERFORM TERMINATION
013500     GOBACK.
013600
013700 INITIALIZATION.
013800     OPEN INPUT INPUT-FILE
013900          OUTPUT REPORT-FILE
014000     WRITE REPORT-RECORD FROM TITLE-HEADING-LINE
014100     PERFORM READ-PAR
014200
014300     ACCEPT REPORT-DATE FROM DATE.
014400
014500 PROCESS-ALL.
014600     PERFORM LOOKUP-MONTH
014700     MOVE INPUT-RECORD TO dl-RECORD-IMAGE
014800     WRITE REPORT-RECORD FROM DETAIL-PRINT-LINE
014900
015000     PERFORM READ-PAR.
015100
015200 TERMINATION.
015300
015400     CLOSE INPUT-FILE
015500           REPORT-FILE.
015600
```

13. SERSRCH1. The Sequential Search

```
015700 READ-PAR.
015800     READ INPUT-FILE
015900     AT END
016000        MOVE 'Y' TO FILE-AT-END
016100     NOT AT END
016200        ADD 1 TO CTR-RECORDS-READ
016300     END-READ.
016500 LOOKUP-MONTH.
016600*   When doing a sequential search,
016700*     you need to set the index to 1 before doing the search
016800*   or else it won't work
016900     SET MONTH-INDEX TO 1
017000*   You search the thing that occurs
017100     SEARCH EACH-MONTH-INFO
017200*   At end means not found
017300     AT END
017400*     Move 'N' to found-switch
017500*     the when is a condition, like an if.
017600*     you must "when" the thing that occurs or an item under it
017700*       comparing it to something on input record (month of hire )
017800     MOVE 'UNKNOWN' TO DL-MONTH-OF-HIRE
017900     WHEN EACH-MONTH-number(MONTH-INDEX) = ER-MONTH-OF-HIRE
018000*     Move 'Y' to found-switch
018100*     at this point you have found it - got a match
018200*     so here is where you do what you need to do on a match
018300       MOVE EACH-MONTH-NAME(month-index) TO DL-MONTH-OF-HIRE
018400       END-SEARCH.
```

13. SERSRCH1. The Sequential Search

The input data file **EMP2**: (the next two lines are a column ruler)

```
         1         2         3         4         5         6
123456789.123456789.123456789.123456789.123456789.123456789.12345678
        01000  PEARLE E GATES           D0001 01 05
        02000  LED BALOON               D0002 04 09
        03000  ORTIZ, DAVID             D0005 06 01
        04000  JOE JONES                D0504 01 12
```

Here is sample JCL:

```
//STEP1     EXEC PGM=SERSRCH1
//STEPLIB DD DSN=your.executable.program.library.here,DISP=SHR
//*  THE NEXT LIBRARY NAME MAY BE DIFFERENT AT YOUR CO
//EMP2      DD   DSN=userid.COBBOOK.DATA(EMP2),DISP=SHR
//REPORTFI  DD   SYSOUT=*
//SYSOUT    DD   SYSOUT=*
//SYSUDUMP  DD   SYSOUT=*
```

The expected output:

```
EMPLOYEE RECORDS WITH MONTH OF HIRE
MAY              01000 PEARLE E GATES        D0001 01 05
SEPTEMBER        02000 LED BALOON            D0002 04 09
JANUARY          03000 ORTIZ, DAVID          D0005 06 01
DECEMBER         04000 JOE JONES             D0504 01 12
```

14. BINSRCH1. The Binary Search

BINSRCH1.
Similar to The Sequential Search, #13 above, but a possibly faster method of searching when large amounts of data are involved. COBOL uses the SEARCH ALL verb.

The binary search can be used when the entries in the table are in strict order, ascending or descending. It may be a good choice and run faster than the sequential search when there are many (over 100 or so) entries in the table.

Do you know what happens if the entries in the table are not in strict order? There will be no compiler diagnostics, no middle of the night abends, but the SEARCH ALL won't work right. It may work for some entries, but not for others, and you may think the program works in every case when it actually doesn't. So the program goes into production and some good records are rejected. After a few complaints, some programmer will be burning the midnight oil trying to track down the source of the problem. Guess who?

Check out your programs carefully. Check the first entry and the last.

14. BINSRCH1. The Binary Search

The program **BINSRCH1:**

```
000200 IDENTIFICATION DIVISION.
000300 PROGRAM-ID. BINSRCH1.
000400* The binary search
000500* reads every input record
000600* after looking up the employee's month of hire on a table,
000700* by a sequential search, it writes it out to an output file
000800 ENVIRONMENT DIVISION.
000900 INPUT-OUTPUT SECTION.
001000 FILE-CONTROL.
001100*     INPUT FILE EMP2
001200     SELECT INPUT-FILE ASSIGN EMP2.
001600*     REPORTFI: A REPORT FILE, PRINTS OUT INFORMATION ON EMPLOYEES
001700*          WITH MONTH OF HIRE, SEND TO PRINTER
001800     SELECT REPORT-FILE ASSIGN REPORTFI.
002200
002300 DATA DIVISION.
002400 FILE SECTION.
002500
002600 FD  INPUT-FILE
002700     RECORDING MODE IS F
003000     RECORD CONTAINS 80 CHARACTERS.
003100 01  INPUT-RECORD.
004700*           INPUT RECORD DESCRIPTION
005000     05  FILLER                      PIC X(08).
005100     05  FILLER                      PIC X(01).
005200     05  ER-EMPLOYEE-NUMBER          PIC X(05).
005300     05  FILLER                      PIC X(01).
005400     05  ER-EMPLOYEE-NAME            PIC X(25).
005500     05  ER-EMPLOYEE-DEPARTMENT      PIC X(05).
005600     05  FILLER                      PIC X(01).
005700     05  ER-EMPLOYEE-SALARY-CODE     PIC X(02).
005800     05  FILLER                      PIC X(01).
005900*    MONTH OF HIRE CAN BE DEFINED AS CHARACTER (ALPHANUMERIC)
006000     05  ER-MONTH-OF-HIRE            PIC X(02).
006100     05  FILLER                      PIC X(29).
003200
```

14. BINSRCH1. The Binary Search

```
003300 FD   REPORT-FILE
003400      RECORDING MODE IS F
003700      RECORD CONTAINS 133 CHARACTERS.
003800
003900 01   REPORT-RECORD                      PIC X(133).
004100 WORKING-STORAGE SECTION.
004200
004300 01   FILE-AT-END          PIC X VALUE 'N'.
004400*
004500 01   SW-VALID-RECORD      PIC X VALUE 'Y'.
004600
006400 01   COUNTERS-AND-ACCUMULATORS.
006500      05  CTR-RECORDS-READ               PIC  9(5)
006600          PACKED-DECIMAL     VALUE 0.
006700      05  CTR-RECORDS-WRITTEN            PIC  9(5)
006800          PACKED-DECIMAL       VALUE 0.
006900
007000 01   TITLE-HEADING-LINE.
007100      05  FILLER                         PIC X(1) VALUE SPACES.
007200      05  FILLER                         PIC X(35)
007300              VALUE 'EMPLOYEE RECORDS WITH MONTH OF HIRE'.
007400      05  FILLER                         PIC X(04) VALUE SPACES.
007500      05  FILLER                         PIC X(33)
007600              VALUE SPACES.
007700      05  REPORT-DATE.
007800          10  REPORT-YY PIC 99.
007900          10  REPORT-MM PIC 99.
008000          10  REPORT-DD PIC 99.
008200 01   DETAIL-PRINT-LINE.
008300      05  FILLER                         PIC X(1) VALUE SPACES.
008400      05  DL-MONTH-OF-HIRE      PIC X(09).
008500      05  DL-RECORD-IMAGE       PIC X(80) VALUE SPACES.
008700 01   MONTH-TABLE-LITERALS.
008800*    This is hard coding a table.
008850*    Examine the code carefully.
009100*    these are fillers, because you
009200*       won't be referring to them directly, by name
009300*    notice how the code (01) is written right
009400*       beside the name (january)
009500*    all the pictures must be the same
009600*    the literals inside of quotes don't have
009700*       to be the same length, but many will code them that way
009800           05      FILLER    PIC X(11)    VALUE '01JANUARY'.
009900           05      FILLER    PIC X(11)    VALUE '02FEBRUARY'.
010000           05      FILLER    PIC X(11)    VALUE '03MARCH'.
010100           05      FILLER    PIC X(11)    VALUE '04APRIL'.
010200           05      FILLER    PIC X(11)    VALUE '05MAY'.
010300           05      FILLER    PIC X(11)    VALUE '06JUNE'.
010400           05      FILLER    PIC X(11)    VALUE '07JULY'.
010500           05      FILLER    PIC X(11)    VALUE '08AUGUST'.
010600           05      FILLER    PIC X(11)    VALUE '09SEPTEMBER'.
010700           05      FILLER    PIC X(11)    VALUE '10OCTOBER'.
010800           05      FILLER    PIC X(11)    VALUE '11NOVEMBER'.
010900           05      FILLER    PIC X(11)    VALUE '12DECEMBER'.
```

```
011000*      Redefines means that this 01 level item
011100*      occupies the same spot in memory as the one it redefines
011200*      so actually the two 01 levels are
011300*      the same thing with different names and different picture
011400 01    MONTH-TABLE REDEFINES MONTH-TABLE-LITERALS.
011500*      Next item must occur as many times
011600*      as there are fillers in the preceding 01
011700*      its picture or the pictures under it
011800*      must add up to the same number as the
011900*      picture in the fillers above (11 in this example)
012000       05    EACH-MONTH-INFO      OCCURS 12 TIMES
012100*      You need the indexed by clause
012200*      if you're going to use the search verb
012300*      this defines and creates the index -
012400*      so no pictures for the index, please
012600*      The ascending (or descending) key clause
012700*      is required for a binary search
012800*      the data must actually be in order
012900*      or this won't work right
013000             ASCENDING KEY IS EACH-month-number
013010             INDEXED BY MONTH-INDEX.
013100
013200         10   EACH-MONTH-NUMBER        PIC XX.
013300         10   EACH-MONTH-NAME          PIC X(09).
013400
013500 PROCEDURE DIVISION.
013600     PERFORM INITIALIZATION
013700     PERFORM PROCESS-ALL UNTIL
013800        FILE-AT-END = 'Y'
013900     PERFORM TERMINATION
014000     GOBACK.
014200 INITIALIZATION.
014300     OPEN INPUT INPUT-FILE
014400          OUTPUT REPORT-FILE
014500     WRITE REPORT-RECORD FROM TITLE-HEADING-LINE
014600     PERFORM READ-PAR
014700**    accept gets today's date from the system
014800     ACCEPT REPORT-DATE FROM DATE.
014900
015000 PROCESS-ALL.
015100     PERFORM LOOKUP-MONTH
015200     MOVE INPUT-RECORD TO dl-reCORD-IMAGE
015300     WRITE REPORT-RECORD FROM DETAIL-PRINT-LINE
015400
015500     PERFORM READ-PAR.
015600
015700 TERMINATION.
015800
015900     CLOSE INPUT-FILE
016000           REPORT-FILE.
016100
016200 READ-PAR.
016300     READ INPUT-FILE
016400     AT END
016500        MOVE 'Y' TO FILE-AT-END
016600     NOT AT END
016700        ADD 1 TO CTR-RECORDS-READ
016800     END-READ.
```

14. BINSRCH1. The Binary Search

```
017000 LOOKUP-MONTH.
017100*   When doing a binary search,
017200*     you don't set the index to 1 before doing the search
017300*   (but if you do, it ignores that and still works)
017400*   you search "all" the thing that occurs,
017500    SEARCH ALL EACH-MONTH-INFO
017600*   At end means not found
017700    AT END
017800*     Move 'N' to found-switch
017900      move 'unknown' to dl-month-of-hire
018000*     the when is a condition, like an if.
018100*     you must "when" the thing that occurs or an item under it
018200*       comparing it to something on input record (month of hire )
018300    WHEN EACH-MONTH-number(MONTH-INDEX) = ER-MONTH-OF-HIRE
018400*     Move 'Y' to found-switch
018500*     at this point you have found it - got a match
018600*     so here is where you do what you need to do on a match
018700       MOVE EACH-MONTH-NAME(month-index) TO DL-MONTH-OF-HIRE
018800    END-SEARCH.
```

The input data file **EMP2**: (the next two lines are a column ruler)

```
         1         2         3         4         5         6
123456789.123456789.123456789.123456789.123456789.123456789.12345678

     01000  PEARLE E GATES          D0001 01
     02000  LED BALOON              D0002 04
     03000  ORTIZ, DAVID            D0005 06
     04000  JOE JONES               D0504 01
```

Here is sample JCL:

```
//STEP1    EXEC PGM=BINSRCH1
//STEPLIB DD DSN=your.executable.program.library.here,DISP=SHR
//*   THE NEXT LIBRARY NAME MAY BE DIFFERENT AT YOUR CO
//EMP2     DD   DSN=userid.COBBOOK.DATA(EMP2),DISP=SHR
//REPORTFI DD   SYSOUT=*
//SYSOUT   DD   SYSOUT=*
//SYSUDUMP DD   SYSOUT=*
```

Expected output:

```
EMPLOYEE RECORDS WITH MONTH OF HIRE
MAY                01000 PEARLE E GATES          D0001 01 05
SEPTEMBER          02000 LED BALOON              D0002 04 09
JANUARY            03000 ORTIZ, DAVID            D0005 06 01
DECEMBER           04000 JOE JONES               D0504 01 12
```

14. BINSRCH1. The Binary Search

This page intentionally left blank

15. LOADTBL1, LOADTBL2. Loading a Table from a Sequential File

LOADTBL1 and LOADTBL2.

The sequential and binary searches you have just seen used a hard-coded COBOL table. In a hard-coded table you type the data in the program. If you want to change anything in the table, you must recompile the entire program and the new program may not be available for use in production for several hours! A more realistic approach is to put the table data in a file, or PDS/PDSE member, then read the data into the program's table. This allows you to change the data without recompiling the program.

Typically, the table data is read in from a member in an PDS/PDSE Someone is assigned the job of keeping this table file up to date. The data will be current and up to date the moment this person saves it and exits from the editor.

The logic to load a table is very similar to that of the first model program presented, the single file program. I will show you that example first: LOADTBL1. Bear in mind that this example does nothing but load the table. Nothing else is done with it. The first program does not produce output, other than some DISPLAY messages.

The second example, LOADTBL2 will do a SEARCH ALL with the table that was just loaded. The program is going to read and do a binary search on a regular (non-table) file. I have coded this program in such a way that the load logic will be very distinct from the logic used to read the regular file.

One point I'd like to make, that is easily missed in all the coding: When doing a binary search, if your table is sorted in ascending order, you'll need to set all the unused entries in the table to high-values. High-values are the highest data value possible in alphanumeric (character datatype) fields. Nothing can be greater than high-values. If you don't set the unused entries to high-values they are set to low-values by default and your binary search won't work! This is shown in the programs LOADTBL1 and LOADTBL2.

Just be aware that this makes high-values a valid data value on the table. If you do a table lookup with a data item (from the input record, usually) that contains high-values it will be marked valid! If you don't want that, you might want to check for high-values in a separate IF statement and reject them.

There are a few things to think about. Later that evening your program will be running in production, at a time when all good programmers should be sound asleep and dreaming of the slopes (snow-covered slopes, not mathematical graph slopes.) Are there more records in the table file than the COBOL OCCURS clause allows? Count the records in the table file. Look at the COBOL OCCURS. Which has a bigger number? It had better be the OCCURS, or you won't get a chance to do any dreaming.

15. LOADTBL1, LOADTBL2. Loading a Table from a Sequential File

The program **LOADTBL1**:

```
000200 IDENTIFICATION DIVISION.
000300 PROGRAM-ID. LOADTBL1.
000400* LOAD A TABLE FROM A SEQUENTIAL FILE
000500* JUST LOAD - DON'T DO ANYTHING ELSE
000600* SEE PROGRAM LOADTBL2 FOR A PROGRAM THAT LOADS AND SEARCHES.
000700 ENVIRONMENT DIVISION.
000800 CONFIGURATION SECTION.
000900 INPUT-OUTPUT SECTION.
001000 FILE-CONTROL.
001100*   INPUT FILE PARTTABL
001200      SELECT TABLE-FILE ASSIGN PARTTABL.
001600 DATA DIVISION.
001700 FILE SECTION.
001800 FD  TABLE-FILE
001810     RECORDING MODE IS F
002000     RECORD CONTAINS 80 CHARACTERS.
002900 01  TABLE-RECORD.
002910     05  WS-TR-PART-NUMBER     PIC X(6).
003000     05  WS-TR-PART-DESC       PIC X(30).
003010     05  FILLER                PIC X(44).
003020
003030 WORKING-STORAGE SECTION.
003050 01 SWITCHES.
004500     05   TABLE-FILE-AT-END    PIC X   VALUE 'N'.
004600     05   INFILE-AT-END        PIC X   VALUE 'N'.
004700     05   VALID-SW             PIC X   VALUE 'Y'.
004800     05   SOMETHING-IN-TABLE   PIC X   VALUE 'N'.
004900     05   TABLE-OVERFLOW       PIC X   VALUE 'N'.
003090
003400 01  PART-TABLE.
003500*    THE 100 USED HERE IS ARBITRARY.
003600*    USE WHATEVER NUMBER YOU NEED FOR THE SIZE OF YOUR TABLE
003700     05  EACH-PART-INFO     OCCURS 100 TIMES
003900         ASCENDING KEY IS EACH-PART-NUMBER
003910         INDEXED BY PART-INDEX.
004000         10  EACH-PART-NUMBER      PIC X(6).
004100         10  EACH-PART-DESCRIPTION PIC X(30).
004200*    THE VALUE OF THE NEXT ITEM MUST BE THE SAME AS THE OCCURS
004300 01  PART-TABLE-MAX-OCCURS PIC S9(5) BINARY VALUE +100.
004400
```

15. LOADTBL1, LOADTBL2. Loading a Table from a Sequential File

```
004500 PROCEDURE DIVISION.
004600     PERFORM TABLE-INITIALIZATION
004700     PERFORM TABLE-PROCESS-ALL
004800         UNTIL TABLE-FILE-AT-END = 'Y'
005000     PERFORM TABLE-TERMINATION
005100     GOBACK.
005200
005300 TABLE-INITIALIZATION.
005400* MOVE HIGH-VALUES SO THAT ALL ENTRIES WILL HAVE THE HIGHEST
005500* VALUE POSSIBLE (LETS SEARCH ALL WORK RIGHT)
005600     MOVE HIGH-VALUES TO PART-TABLE
005700     SET PART-INDEX TO 1
005800     OPEN INPUT TABLE-FILE
005900     PERFORM TABLE-READ-PAR.
006000
006100 TABLE-PROCESS-ALL.
006110     IF PART-INDEX > PART-TABLE-MAX-OCCURS
006120     THEN
006130        MOVE 'Y' TO TABLE-FILE-AT-END
006140        MOVE 'Y' TO TABLE-OVERFLOW
006150          DISPLAY 'INDEX GT MAX'
006160     ELSE
006170        MOVE TABLE-RECORD TO EACH-PART-INFO(PART-INDEX)
006180        MOVE 'Y' TO SOMETHING-IN-TABLE
006190        SET PART-INDEX UP BY 1
006191********  DISPLAY 'INDEX NOT GT MAX'
006192          PERFORM TABLE-READ-PAR
006193     END-IF.
006500
```

15. LOADTBL1, LOADTBL2. Loading a Table from a Sequential File

```
006600 TABLE-TERMINATION.
006700*     AT THIS POINT CHECK TO SEE IF THE TABLE
006800*     WAS PROPERLY LOADED
006910     IF TABLE-OVERFLOW = 'Y'
006920     THEN
006930         DISPLAY 'MORE RECORDS THAN TABLE ENTRIES'
006940         GO TO ERROR-EXIT
006950     END-IF
006960
006970     IF SOMETHING-IN-TABLE = 'Y'
006980     THEN
006990         DISPLAY 'TABLE APPEARS TO BE LOADED OK'
006991     ELSE
006992         DISPLAY 'NOTHING LOADED IN TABLE'
006993         GO TO ERROR-EXIT
006994     END-IF
006995
006998*     THE NEXT IS NOT A REQUIRMENT.
006999*     IT DISPLAYS ALL THE ENTRIES IN THE TABLE - JUST TO SHOW
007000*     IF IT WORKED PROPERLY
007001     DISPLAY 'HERE IS THE TABLE AFTER LOADING'
007002     PERFORM
007003         VARYING PART-INDEX FROM 1 BY 1
007004         UNTIL    PART-INDEX > PART-TABLE-MAX-OCCURS
007005
007006         DISPLAY EACH-PART-NUMBER (PART-INDEX)
007007                 EACH-PART-DESCRIPTION (PART-INDEX)
007008     END-PERFORM
007009
007800       CLOSE TABLE-FILE.
007900
008000 TABLE-READ-PAR.
008100     READ TABLE-FILE
008200         AT END MOVE 'Y' TO TABLE-FILE-AT-END
008300     END-READ.
008310
008400 ERROR-EXIT.
008500*     DISPLAY MESSAGES IF NEEDED
008700*     END THE PROGRAM
008800       GOBACK.
```

15. LOADTBL1, LOADTBL2. Loading a Table from a Sequential File

The input data file **PARTTABL**: (the next two lines are a column ruler)

```
         1         2         3         4         5         6
123456789.123456789.123456789.123456789.123456789.123456789.12345678

PART01 LEFT HANDED WIDGET WRENCHES
PART02 LEAD-WINGED GLIDERS
PART04 LEFT FOOT REEBOKS
PART06 286 COMPUTERS W 4K HARD DISK
```

Here is sample JCL:

```
//STEP1     EXEC PGM=LOADTBL1
//STEPLIB DD DSN=your.executable.program.library.here,DISP=SHR
//*   THE NEXT LIBRARY NAME MAY BE DIFFERENT AT YOUR CO
//PARTTABL   DD    DSN=userid.COBBOOK.DATA(PARTTABL),DISP=SHR
//SYSOUT     DD    SYSOUT=*
//SYSUDUMP   DD    SYSOUT=*
```

Display messages produced by the program. To file "SYSOUT".
```
TABLE APPEARS TO BE LOADED OK
HERE IS THE TABLE AFTER LOADING
PART01 LEFT HANDED WIDGET WRENCHES
PART02 LEAD-WINGED GLIDERS
PART04 LEFT FOOT REEBOKS
PART06 286 COMPUTERS W 4K HARD DISK
```

15. LOADTBL1, LOADTBL2. Loading a Table from a Sequential File

The program **LOADTBL2**:

```
000200 IDENTIFICATION DIVISION.
000300 PROGRAM-ID. LOADTBL2.
000400* Load a table from a sequential file
000500* read a regular file
000600* check each record to see if it has a valid part number
000700 ENVIRONMENT DIVISION.
000800 CONFIGURATION SECTION.
000900 INPUT-OUTPUT SECTION.
001000 FILE-CONTROL.
001100*      TABLE FILE PARTTABL
001200      SELECT TABLE-FILE  ASSIGN PARTTABL.
001600*     REGULAR INPUT FILE PARTS1
001700      SELECT INFILE      ASSIGN PARTS1.
002100 DATA DIVISION.
002200 FILE SECTION.
002300 FD   TABLE-FILE
002310      RECORDING MODE IS F
002700      RECORD CONTAINS 80 CHARACTERS.
002800 01   TABLE-RECORD.
004500      05   WS-TR-PART-NUMBER    PIC X(6).
004600      05   WS-TR-PART-DESC      PIC X(30).
004700      05   FILLER               PIC X(44).
004800
003000 FD   INFILE
003010      RECORDING MODE IS F
003410      RECORD CONTAINS 80 CHARACTERS.
003500 01   INFILE-RECORD.
005000*      PICTURES MUST CORRESPOND TO THE ACTUAL INPUT FILE
005100      05   PART-NUMBER          PIC X(6).
005200      05   PART-DESCR           PIC X(30).
005300      05   QTY-ON-HAND          PIC 9(3).
005400      05   QTY-ON-ORDER         PIC 9(3).
005500      05   QTY-ON-RESERVE       PIC 9(3).
005600      05   PART-PRICE           PIC 9(3)V99.
005700      05   UNUSED               PIC X(30).
005800
003700 WORKING-STORAGE SECTION.
003800 01   SWITCHES.
003900      05   TABLE-FILE-AT-END    PIC X   VALUE 'N'.
004000      05   INFILE-AT-END        PIC X   VALUE 'N'.
004100      05   VALID-SW             PIC X   VALUE 'Y'.
004210      05   SOMETHING-IN-TABLE      VALUE 'N'      PIC X.
004220      05   TABLE-OVERFLOW          VALUE 'N'      PIC X.
004300
005900 01 PART-TABLE.
006000*      The 100 used here is arbitrary.
006010      05   EACH-PART-INFO     OCCURS 100 TIMES
006020           ASCENDING KEY IS EACH-PART-NUMBER
006030           INDEXED BY PART-INDEX.
006040           10   EACH-PART-NUMBER      PIC X(6).
006050           10   EACH-PART-DESCRIPTION PIC X(30).
006060*      THE VALUE OF THE NEXT ITEM MUST BE THE SAME AS THE OCCURS AB
006070 01   PART-TABLE-MAX-OCCURS PIC S9(5) BINARY VALUE +100.
006900
```

15. LOADTBL1, LOADTBL2. Loading a Table from a Sequential File

```
007000 PROCEDURE DIVISION.
007100     PERFORM TABLE-INITIALIZATION
007200     PERFORM TABLE-PROCESS-ALL
007300         UNTIL TABLE-FILE-AT-END = 'Y'
007500     PERFORM TABLE-TERMINATION
007600     PERFORM INFILE-INITIALIZATION
007700     PERFORM INFILE-PROCESS-ALL
007800         UNTIL INFILE-AT-END = 'Y'
007900     PERFORM INFILE-TERMINATION
008000     GOBACK.
008100
008200 TABLE-INITIALIZATION.
008300*    See text for explanation of next move
008400     MOVE HIGH-VALUES TO PART-TABLE
008500*    Absolutely must set the index to 1
008600*        an index does not have a default initial value
008700*        and you are not allowed to set an index to 0
008800     SET PART-INDEX TO 1
008900     OPEN INPUT TABLE-FILE
009000     PERFORM TABLE-READ-PAR.
009100
009200 TABLE-PROCESS-ALL.
009300     IF PART-INDEX > PART-TABLE-MAX-OCCURS
009400     THEN
009500        MOVE 'Y' TO TABLE-FILE-AT-END
009600        MOVE 'Y' TO TABLE-OVERFLOW
009610          DISPLAY 'INDEX GT MAX'
009620     ELSE
009630        MOVE TABLE-RECORD TO EACH-PART-INFO(PART-INDEX)
009640        MOVE 'Y' TO SOMETHING-IN-TABLE
009650        SET PART-INDEX UP BY 1
009660********  DISPLAY 'INDEX NOT GT MAX'
009670        PERFORM TABLE-READ-PAR
009680     END-IF.
```

15. LOADTBL1, LOADTBL2. Loading a Table from a Sequential File

```
009800 TABLE-TERMINATION.
009900*     AT THIS POINT CHECK TO SEE IF THE TABLE
010000*     WAS PROPERLY LOADED
010100      IF TABLE-OVERFLOW = 'Y'
010200      THEN
010300         DISPLAY 'MORE RECORDS THAN TABLE ENTRIES'
010400         GO TO ERROR-EXIT
010500      END-IF
010700      IF SOMETHING-IN-TABLE = 'Y'
010800      THEN
010900         DISPLAY 'TABLE APPEARS TO BE LOADED OK'
011000      ELSE
011100         DISPLAY 'NOTHING LOADED IN TABLE'
011200         GO TO ERROR-EXIT
011210      END-IF
011230*     DISPLAY 'READ ' INPUT-RECORD-COUNT 'RECORDS'
011250*     NEXT IS NOT REQUIRED
011260*     IT DISPLAYS ALL THE ENTRIES IN THE TABLE - JUST TO SHOW
011270*     IF IT WORKED PROPERLY
011280      DISPLAY 'HERE IS THE TABLE AFTER LOADING'
011290      PERFORM
011291         VARYING PART-INDEX FROM 1 BY 1
011292         UNTIL   PART-INDEX > PART-TABLE-MAX-OCCURS
011294         DISPLAY EACH-PART-NUMBER (PART-INDEX)
011295                 EACH-PART-DESCRIPTION (PART-INDEX)
011296      END-PERFORM
011307
011308       CLOSE TABLE-FILE.
011310
```

15. LOADTBL1, LOADTBL2. Loading a Table from a Sequential File

```
011400 TABLE-READ-PAR.
011500     READ TABLE-FILE
011600         AT END MOVE 'Y' TO TABLE-FILE-AT-END
011700     END-READ.
011800
011900 INFILE-INITIALIZATION.
012000     OPEN INPUT INFILE
012100     PERFORM INFILE-READ-PAR.
012200
012300 INFILE-PROCESS-ALL.
012400     MOVE 'Y' TO VALID-SW
012500     PERFORM TABLE-LOOKUP
012600     IF VALID-SW = 'Y'
012700*        Not doing much of anything here in this program
012800*        but you could write out records,
012900*        print lines in report, etc
013000         DISPLAY 'GOOD RECORD' INFILE-RECORD
013100     ELSE
013200         DISPLAY 'BAD RECORD' INFILE-RECORD
013300     END-IF
013400     PERFORM infile-READ-PAR.
013500
013600 INFILE-TERMINATION.
013700     CLOSE INFILE.
013800
013900 INFILE-READ-PAR.
014000     READ INFILE
014100         AT END MOVE 'Y' TO infile-AT-END
014200     END-READ.
014300
014400 TABLE-LOOKUP.
014500* This is a binary search,
014600* but a sequential search could have been used
014700     IF PART-NUMBER IS EQUAL TO HIGH-VALUES
014800     THEN MOVE 'N' TO VALID-SW
014900     ELSE
015000         SEARCH ALL EACH-PART-INFO
015100         AT END
015200*         DISPLAY INPUT-PART 'NOT FOUND'
015300         MOVE 'N' TO VALID-SW
015400         WHEN EACH-PART-NUMBER(PART-INDEX) = PART-NUMBER
015500*         DISPLAY INPUT-STATE 'FOUND'
015600         MOVE EACH-PART-DESCRIPTION(PART-INDEX)
015700             TO PART-DESCR
015900         END-SEARCH
016000     END-IF.
016100
016200 ERROR-EXIT.
016300*    DISPLAY MESSAGES IF NEEDED
016400*    END THE PROGRAM
016500     GOBACK.
```

15. LOADTBL1, LOADTBL2. Loading a Table from a Sequential File

The input data file **PARTTABL**: (the next two lines are a column ruler)

```
         1         2         3         4         5         6
123456789.123456789.123456789.123456789.123456789.123456789.12345678

PART01 LEFT HANDED WIDGET WRENCHES
PART02 LEAD-WINGED GLIDERS
PART04 LEFT FOOT REEBOKS
PART06 286 COMPUTERS W 4K HARD DISK
```

The input data file **PARTS1**: (the next two lines are a column ruler)

```
         1         2         3         4         5         6
123456789.123456789.123456789.123456789.123456789.123456789.12345678

PART01                              003 007 002 10022
PART02                              004 006 001 14054
PART04                              021 002 004 04323
PART06                              043 077 012 00042
```

Here is sample JCL:

```
//STEP1     EXEC PGM=LOADTBL2
//STEPLIB DD DSN=your.executable.program.library.here,DISP=SHR
//*   THE NEXT LIBRARY NAME MAY BE DIFFERENT AT YOUR CO
//PARTTABL   DD    DSN=userid.COBBOOK.DATA(PARTTABL),DISP=SHR
//PARTS1     DD    DSN=userid.COBBOOK.DATA(PARTS1),DISP=SHR
//SYSOUT     DD    SYSOUT=*
//SYSUDUMP   DD    SYSOUT=*
```

Expected output:
```
GOOD RECORDPART01 LEFT HANDED WIDGET WRENCHES     003 007 002 10022
GOOD RECORDPART02 LEAD-WINGED GLIDERS             004 006 001 14054
GOOD RECORDPART04 LEFT FOOT REEBOKS               021 002 004 04323
GOOD RECORDPART06 286 COMPUTERS W 4K HARD DISK    043 077 012 00042
```

16. VSAMSEQ1, VSAMSEQ2. The VSAM File Read Sequentially

VSAMSEQ1 and VSAMSEQ2.

These two programs are identical, except that VSAMSEQ2 uses the optional VSAM extended status codes for error checking.

We have a VSAM KSDS (Key Sequenced Data Set) as input. This file can be read randomly or sequentially. In this first VSAM program we will read it sequentially. We are treating it like an ordinary sequential file, or like a VSAM ESDS (Entry Sequenced Data Set).

You might need to produce a report using the VSAM file. The report will assume that the file is sorted. When reading a KSDS sequentially you will see the records in order, as if they had been sorted. You can do a program with subtotals, provided that the data is actually in sequence by all the fields needed for the subtotals. The VSAM KSDS might be a transaction file or a master file used in a file update program. This is possible because the records will appear in order.

This program will get you familiar with the simple JCL needed for any VSAM file (just DSNAME and DISP.) You will see what the COBOL SELECT statements look like as well as with status code checking.

16. VSAMSEQ1, VSAMSEQ2. The VSAM File Read Sequentially

The program **VSAMSEQ1:**

```
000100 IDENTIFICATION DIVISION.
000200 PROGRAM-ID. VSAMSEQ1.
000300* READ VSAM KSDS SEQUENTIALLY
000400* JUST DISPLAY THE VSAM RECORDS
000500* NOTHING COMPLEX IN THIS PROGRAM
000600* THE LOGIC IS THE SAME AS FOR THE SIMPLE FILE READ SEQUENTIALLY
000700 ENVIRONMENT DIVISION.
000800 CONFIGURATION SECTION.
000900 INPUT-OUTPUT SECTION.
001000 FILE-CONTROL.
001100*     INPUT VSAM FILE IS: userid.VSAMKSDS.EMPSORTD
001200*
001300*     USES EMPSORTD INPUT TO JCL
001400*      THE NAMES MAY BE DIFFERENT AT YOUR COMPANY
001500     SELECT VSAM-KSDS-FILE ASSIGN VSAMKSDS
001600        ORGANIZATION IS INDEXED
001700        ACCESS MODE IS SEQUENTIAL
001800*     RECORD KEY NOT NEEDED FOR SEQ READING
001900        RECORD KEY IS VSAM-KSDS-RECORD-KEY
002000        FILE STATUS  IS VSAM-STATUS-CODE
002100                        VSAM-EXTENDED-STATUS-CODE.
002200 DATA DIVISION.
002300 FILE SECTION.
002400
002500 FD  VSAM-KSDS-FILE.
002600 01  VSAM-KSDS-RECORD.
002700*     YOU WON'T BE USING THE NEXT FIELD IN THIS PROGRAM
002800*     BECAUSE YOU ARE READING SEQUENTIALLY, NOT RANDOMLY
002900*     THE 20 MEANS THE KEY FIELD HAS A LENGTH OF 20
003000*     REFER  BACK TO THE JCL WHICH CREATES THE VSAM FILE
003100*     BECAUSE THAT IS WHERE THE 20 COMES FROM
003200*     THE RECORD KEY IS ACTUALLY EMPLOYEE NAME IN THIS DATA FILE
003300     05  VSAM-KSDS-RECORD-KEY    PIC X(20).
003400     05  VSAM-KSDS-EMP-INFO      PIC X(60).
```

16. VSAMSEQ1, VSAMSEQ2. The VSAM File Read Sequentially

```
003600 WORKING-STORAGE SECTION.
003700 01  VSAM-STATUS-CODE.
003800     05 VSAM-STATUS-CODE-BYTE1    PIC X.
003900     05 VSAM-STATUS-CODE-BYTE2    PIC X.
004000
004100 01  VSAM-EXTENDED-STATUS-CODE.
004200     05 VSAM-EXTENDED-RETURN-CODE   PIC S9(4) COMP.
004300     05 VSAM-EXTENDED-FUNCTION-CODE PIC S9(4) COMP.
004400     05 VSAM-EXTENDED-FEEDBACK-CODE PIC S9(4) COMP.
004500
004600 01  SWITCHES.
004700      05  FILE-AT-END    PIC X  VALUE 'N'.
004900 PROCEDURE DIVISION.
005000     PERFORM INITIALIZATION
005100     PERFORM PROCESS-ALL
005200         UNTIL FILE-AT-END = 'Y'
005300     PERFORM TERMINATION
005400     GOBACK.
005600 INITIALIZATION.
005700     OPEN INPUT VSAM-KSDS-FILE
005800     IF VSAM-STATUS-CODE IS NOT EQUAL TO '00'
005900     THEN GO TO ERROR-EXIT
006000     END-IF
006100     PERFORM READ-PAR.
006300 PROCESS-ALL.
006400*    THIS PROGRAM IS SIMPLE.
006500*    IT JUST DISPLAYS THE RECORDS OF THE VSAM FILE
006600*    OTHER PROGRAMS WOULD DO MORE INVOLVED PROCESSING
006700     DISPLAY VSAM-KSDS-RECORD
006800     PERFORM READ-PAR.
006900
007000 TERMINATION.
007100     CLOSE VSAM-KSDS-FILE.
007300 READ-PAR.
007400     READ VSAM-KSDS-FILE
007500     AT END MOVE 'Y' TO FILE-AT-END
007600     NOT AT END
007700      IF VSAM-STATUS-CODE IS NOT EQUAL TO '00'
007800      THEN GO TO ERROR-EXIT
007900      END-IF
008000     END-READ.
008200 ERROR-EXIT.
008300*    SEE THE PROGRAM VSAMSEQ2 FOR VSAM STATUS CODES
008400*    AND EXTENDED STATUS CODES
008500*    AND THE REMAINDER OF THIS PARAGRAPH
008550     GOBACK.
```

The data that is input to IDCAMS which creates *userid*.**VSAMKSDS.EMPSORTD**

You have uploaded it and placed it in member *userid*.COBBOOK.DATA(EMPSORTD)

```
          1         2         3         4         5         6
123456789.123456789.123456789.123456789.123456789.123456789.12345678

BUD WEIZER           05000  9  0001  0000001  000000
HERB GARDNER         03000  1  0040  0000055  000022
HUGH MUNGUS          06000  1  0200  0000020  000020
L. A. CALIFORNIA     07000  5  0020  0000033  000033
PAT SULLIVAN         04000  0  0002  0000022  000011
PEARLE E. GATES      01000  2  0010  0000020  000300
PHIL HARMONIC        02000  3  0030  0000050  000020
```

16. VSAMSEQ1, VSAMSEQ2. The VSAM File Read Sequentially

Here is sample JCL:

```
//* vsamseq1.jcl
//DEFKSDS   EXEC PGM=IDCAMS
//SYSPRINT DD    SYSOUT=*
//SYSIN    DD    *
 DELETE (userid.VSAMKSDS.EMPSORTD) CLUSTER

 DEFINE CLUSTER -
 (NAME(userid.VSAMKSDS.EMPSORTD) -
  CYLINDERS(1,1) -
  KEYS(20,0) -
  RECORDSIZE(80,80) -
  VOLUMES(insert a volume serial number here) -
  INDEXED )

 REPRO INFILE(INFILE) OUTDATASET(userid.VSAMKSDS.EMPSORTD)

/*
//INFILE DD   DSN=userid.COBBOOK.DATA(EMPSORTD),DISP=SHR
//*
//STEP1     EXEC PGM=VSAMSEQ1
//STEPLIB DD DSN=your.executable.program.library.here,DISP=SHR
//*   THE NEXT DATASET NAME MAY BE DIFFERENT AT YOUR CO
//VSAMKSDS   DD   DSN=userid.VSAMKSDS.EMPSORTD,DISP=SHR
//SYSOUT    DD    SYSOUT=*
//SYSUDUMP  DD    SYSOUT=*
//SYSABOUT  DD    SYSOUT=*
//SYSDBOUT  DD    SYSOUT=*
//*
```

Expected output:
```
BUD WEIZER            05000  9  0001  0000001  000000
HERB GARDNER          03000  1  0040  0000055  000022
HUGH MUNGUS           06000  1  0200  0000020  000020
L. A. CALIFORNIA      07000  5  0020  0000033  000033
PAT SULLIVAN          04000  0  0002  0000022  000011
PEARLE E. GATES       01000  2  0010  0000020  000300
PHIL HARMONIC         02000  3  0030  0000050  000020
```

16. VSAMSEQ1, VSAMSEQ2. The VSAM File Read Sequentially

The program **VSAMSEQ2:**

```
000100 IDENTIFICATION DIVISION.
000200 PROGRAM-ID. VSAMSEQ2.
000300*  THIS PROGRAM IS THE SAME AS VSAMSEQ1,
000400*   EXCEPT THAT THIS ONE USES EXTENDED VSAM STATUS CODES.
000500* READ VSAM KSDS SEQUENTIALLY
000600* JUST DISPLAY THE VSAM RECORDS
000700* NOTHING COMPLEX IN THIS PROGRAM
000800* THE LOGIC IS THE SAME AS FOR THE SIMPLE FILE READ SEQUENTIALLY
000900 ENVIRONMENT DIVISION.
001000 CONFIGURATION SECTION.
001100 INPUT-OUTPUT SECTION.
001200 FILE-CONTROL.
001300*    INPUT VSAM FILE IS: userid.VSAMKSDS.EMPSORTD
001400*
001500*    USES EMPSORTD AS INPUT TO JCL
001600*    THE NAMES MAY BE DIFFERENT AT YOUR COMPANY
001700     SELECT VSAM-KSDS-FILE ASSIGN VSAMKSDS
001800        ORGANIZATION IS INDEXED
001900        ACCESS MODE IS SEQUENTIAL
002000*    RECORD KEY NOT NEEDED FOR SEQ READING
002100        RECORD KEY IS VSAM-KSDS-RECORD-KEY
002200        FILE STATUS  IS VSAM-STATUS-CODE
002300                        VSAM-EXTENDED-STATUS-CODE.
002400 DATA DIVISION.
002500 FILE SECTION.
002600
002700 FD  VSAM-KSDS-FILE.
002800 01  VSAM-KSDS-RECORD.
002900*    YOU WON'T BE USING THE NEXT FIELD IN THIS PROGRAM
003000*    BECAUSE YOU ARE READING SEQUENTIALLY, NOT RANDOMLY
003100*    THE 20 MEANS THE KEY FIELD HAS A LENGTH OF 20
003200*    REFER  BACK TO THE JCL WHICH CREATES THE VSAM FILE
003300*    BECAUSE THAT IS WHERE THE 20 COMES FROM
003400*    THE RECORD KEY IS ACTUALLY EMPLOYEE NAME IN THIS DATA FILE
003500     05  VSAM-KSDS-RECORD-KEY    PIC X(20).
003600     05  VSAM-KSDS-EMP-INFO      PIC X(60).
003700
003800
003900 WORKING-STORAGE SECTION.
004000
004100 01  VSAM-STATUS-CODE.
004200     05 VSAM-STATUS-CODE-BYTE1   PIC X.
004300     05 VSAM-STATUS-CODE-BYTE2   PIC X.
004400
004500 01  VSAM-EXTENDED-STATUS-CODE.
004600     05 VSAM-EXTENDED-RETURN-CODE    PIC S9(4) COMP.
004700     05 VSAM-EXTENDED-FUNCTION-CODE PIC S9(4) COMP.
004800     05 VSAM-EXTENDED-FEEDBACK-CODE PIC S9(4) COMP.
004900
005000 01  SWITCHES.
005100     05  FILE-AT-END     PIC X  VALUE 'N'.
```

16. VSAMSEQ1, VSAMSEQ2. The VSAM File Read Sequentially

```
005300 PROCEDURE DIVISION.
005400     PERFORM INITIALIZATION
005500     PERFORM PROCESS-ALL
005600         UNTIL FILE-AT-END = 'Y'
005700     PERFORM TERMINATION
005800     GOBACK.
005900
006000 INITIALIZATION.
006100     OPEN INPUT VSAM-KSDS-FILE
006200     IF VSAM-STATUS-CODE IS NOT EQUAL TO '00'
006220         THEN PERFORM EVALUATE-VSAM-STATUS-CODE
006230             GO TO ERROR-EXIT
006240         END-IF
006400     END-IF
006500     PERFORM READ-PAR.
006600
006700 PROCESS-ALL.
006800*    THIS PROGRAM IS SIMPLE.
006900*    IT JUST DISPLAYS THE RECORDS OF THE VSAM FILE
007000*    OTHER PROGRAMS WOULD DO MORE INVOLVED PROCESSING
007100     DISPLAY VSAM-KSDS-RECORD
007200     PERFORM READ-PAR.
007300
007400 TERMINATION.
007500     CLOSE VSAM-KSDS-FILE.
007600
007700 READ-PAR.
007800     READ VSAM-KSDS-FILE
007900     AT END MOVE 'Y' TO FILE-AT-END
008000     NOT AT END
008100       IF VSAM-STATUS-CODE IS NOT EQUAL TO '00'
008200       THEN GO TO ERROR-EXIT
008300       END-IF
008400     END-READ.
008500
```

```
008600 EVALUATE-VSAM-STATUS-CODE.
008700*     THIS WILL DISPLAY DIAGNOSTIC MESSAGES
008800*     FOR VSAM STATUS CODES AS WELL AS ORDINARY SEQUENTIAL
008900     DISPLAY 'FILE STATUS CODE:' VSAM-STATUS-CODE
009000     EVALUATE VSAM-STATUS-CODE
009100     WHEN '00' DISPLAY 'SUCCESSFUL COMPLETION'
009200     WHEN '02' DISPLAY 'DUPLICATE KEY, NON UNIQ. ALT INDX'
009300     WHEN '04' DISPLAY 'READ, WRONG LENGTH RECORD'
009400     WHEN '05' DISPLAY 'OPEN, FILE NOT PRESENT'
009500     WHEN '07' DISPLAY 'CLOSE OPTION INCOMPAT FILE DEVICE'
009600               DISPLAY 'OPEN IMPLIES TAPE; TAPE NOT USED'
009700     WHEN '10' DISPLAY 'END OF FILE'
009800     WHEN '14' DISPLAY 'RRN > RELATIVE KEY DATA'
009900     WHEN '20' DISPLAY 'INVALID KEY VSAM KSDS OR RRDS'
010000     WHEN '21' DISPLAY 'SEQUENCE ERROR, ON WRITE'
010100               DISPLAY 'OR CHANGING KEY ON REWRITE'
010200     WHEN '22' DISPLAY 'DUPLICATE KEY'
010300     WHEN '23' DISPLAY 'RECORD OR FILE NOT FOUND'
010400     WHEN '24' DISPLAY 'BOUNDARY VIOLATION.'
010500               DISPLAY 'WRITE PAST END OF KSDS RECORD '
010600               DISPLAY 'COBOL 370: REL: REC# TOO BIG'
010700               DISPLAY 'OUT OF SPACE ON KSDS/RRDS FILE'
010800     WHEN '30' DISPLAY 'PERMANENT DATA ERROR'
010900               DISPLAY 'DATA CHECK, PARITY CHK, HARDW'
011000     WHEN '34' DISPLAY 'BOUNDARY VIOLATION'
011100               DISPLAY 'WRITE PAST END OF ESDS RECORD'
011200               DISPLAY 'OR NO SPACE TO ADD KSDS/RRDS RECORD'
011300               DISPLAY 'OUT OF SPACE ON SEQUENTIAL FILE'
011400     WHEN '35' DISPLAY 'OPEN, FILE NOT PRESENT'
011500     WHEN '37' DISPLAY 'OPEN MODE INCOMPAT WITH DEVICE'
011600     WHEN '38' DISPLAY 'OPENING FILE CLOSED WITH LOCK'
011700     WHEN '39' DISPLAY 'OPEN, FILE ATTRIB CONFLICTING'
011800     WHEN '41' DISPLAY 'OPEN, FILE IS OPEN'
011900     WHEN '42' DISPLAY 'CLOSE, FILE IS CLOSED'
012000     WHEN '43' DISPLAY 'DELETE OR REWRITE & NO GOOD READ FIRST'
012100     WHEN '44' DISPLAY 'BOUNDARY VIOLATION/REWRITE REC TOO BIG'
012200     WHEN '46' DISPLAY 'SEQUENTIAL READ WITHOUT POSITIONING'
012300     WHEN '47' DISPLAY 'READING FILE NOT OPEN AS INPUT/IO/EXTEND'
012400     WHEN '48' DISPLAY 'WRITE WITHOUT OPEN IO'
012500     WHEN '49' DISPLAY 'DELETE OR REWRITE WITHOUT OPEN IO'
012600     WHEN '90' DISPLAY 'UNKNOWN'
012700     WHEN '91' DISPLAY 'VSAM - PASSWORD FAILURE'
012800     WHEN '92' DISPLAY 'LOGIC ERROR/OPENING AN OPEN FILE'
012900               DISPLAY 'OR READING OUTPUT FILE'
013000               DISPLAY 'OR WRITE INPUT FILE'
013100               DISPLAY 'OR DEL/REW BUT NO PRIOR READ'
013200     WHEN '93' DISPLAY 'VSAM - VIRTSTOR. RESOURCE NOT AVAILABLE'
013300     WHEN '94' DISPLAY 'VSAM - SEQUENTIAL READ AFTER END OF FILE'
013400               DISPLAY 'OR NO CURRENT REC POINTER FOR SEQ'
013500     WHEN '95' DISPLAY 'VSAM - INVALID FILE INFORMATION'
013600               DISPLAY 'OR OPEN OUTPUT (LOAD) '
013700               DISPLAY  'WITH FILE THAT NEVER CONTNED DATA'
013710               DISPLAY  'OR ESDS OPEND OUTPUT BUT CONTNS DATA'
013800     WHEN '96' DISPLAY 'VSAM - MISSING DD STATEMENT IN JCL'
013900     WHEN '97' DISPLAY 'VSAM - OPEN OK, FILE INTEGRITY VERIFIED'
014000               DISPLAY 'FILE SHOULD BE OK'
014100     WHEN OTHER DISPLAY 'UNKNOWN REASON' VSAM-STATUS-CODE
014200     END-EVALUATE.
```

16. VSAMSEQ1, VSAMSEQ2. The VSAM File Read Sequentially

```
014300*    additional code in case you need it
014500*    commercial use or resale of this document is not permitted
014400     EVALUATE VSAM-EXTENDED-RETURN-CODE
014500     WHEN 0 DISPLAY 'SUCCESSFUL COMPLETION'
014600     WHEN 4 DISPLAY 'ANOTHER REQUEST IS ACTIVE'
014700     WHEN 8 DISPLAY 'THERE IS A LOGICAL ERROR'
014800            PERFORM EVALUATE-LOGICAL-ERROR
014900     WHEN 12 DISPLAY 'THERE IS A PHYSICAL ERROR'
015000            PERFORM EVALUATE-PHYSICAL-ERROR
015100     WHEN OTHER DISPLAY 'UNKNOWN REASON'
015200     END-EVALUATE.
015300
015400 EVALUATE-VSAM-EXTENDED.
015500     EVALUATE VSAM-EXTENDED-FUNCTION-CODE
015600     WHEN 0 DISPLAY 'ACCESSING BASE CLUSTER, NO PROBLEM'
015700     WHEN 1 DISPLAY 'ACCESSING BASE CLUSTER, MAY BE A PROBLEM'
015800     WHEN 2 DISPLAY 'ACCESSING ALTERNATE INDEX, NO PROBLEM'
015900     WHEN 3 DISPLAY 'ACCESSING ALTERNATE INDEX, MAY BE A PROBLEM'
016000     WHEN 4 DISPLAY 'UPGRADE PROCESSING, NO PROBLEM'
016100     WHEN 5 DISPLAY 'UPGRADE PROCESSING, MAY BE A PROBLEM'
016200     WHEN OTHER DISPLAY 'UNKNOWN REASON'
016300     END-EVALUATE.
016400
016500 EVALUATE-PHYSICAL-ERROR.
016600*    USE THIS WHEN THERE IS RC 12 IN VSAM-EXTENDED-RETURN-CODE
016700     EVALUATE VSAM-EXTENDED-FEEDBACK-CODE
016800     WHEN 4 DISPLAY 'READ ERROR ON DATA'
016900     WHEN 8 DISPLAY 'READ ERROR ON INDEX'
017000     WHEN 12 DISPLAY 'READ ERROR IN SEQUENCE SET'
017100     WHEN 16 DISPLAY 'WRITE ERROR ON DATA'
017200     WHEN 20 DISPLAY 'WRITE ERROR ON INDEX'
017300     WHEN 24 DISPLAY 'WRITE ERROR IN SEQUENCE SET'
017400     WHEN OTHER DISPLAY 'UNKNOWN REASON'
017400     END-EVALUATE.
```

16. VSAMSEQ1, VSAMSEQ2. The VSAM File Read Sequentially

```
017700   EVALUATE-LOGICAL-ERROR.
017800*     USE THIS WHEN THERE IS RC  8 IN VSAM-EXTENDED-RETURN-CODE
017900     EVALUATE VSAM-EXTENDED-FEEDBACK-CODE
018000       WHEN    4 DISPLAY 'READ PAST END OF FILE'
018100       WHEN    8 DISPLAY 'DUPLICATE KEY'
018200       WHEN   12 DISPLAY 'KEY SEQUENCE ERROR'
018300       WHEN   16 DISPLAY 'NOT FOUND'
018400       WHEN   20 DISPLAY 'CONTROL INTERVAL IN USE BY OTHER JOB'
018500       WHEN   24 DISPLAY 'VOLUME CANNOT BE MOUNTED'
018600       WHEN   28 DISPLAY 'UNABLE TO EXTEND DATASET'
018700       WHEN   32 DISPLAY 'RBA NOT FOUND'
018800       WHEN   36 DISPLAY 'KEY IS NOT IN A DEFINED KEY RANGE'
018900       WHEN   40 DISPLAY 'INSUFFICIENT VIRTUAL STORAGE'
019000       WHEN   64 DISPLAY 'NO AVAILABLE STRINGS'
019100       WHEN   68 DISPLAY 'OPEN DID NOT SPECIFY PROC TYPE'
019200       WHEN   72 DISPLAY 'KEY ACCESS TO ESDS OR RRDS'
019300       WHEN   76 DISPLAY 'ATTEMPTED INSERT TO WRONG TYPE DATASET'
019400       WHEN   80 DISPLAY 'ATTEMPTED DELETE FROM ESDS'
019500       WHEN   84 DISPLAY 'OPTCD LOC FOR PUT REQUEST'
019600       WHEN   88 DISPLAY 'POSITION NOT ESTABLISHED'
019700       WHEN   92 DISPLAY 'PUT WITHOUT GET FOR UPDATE'
019800       WHEN   96 DISPLAY 'TRYING TO CHANGE PRIMARY KEY'
019900       WHEN  100 DISPLAY 'TRYING TO CHANGE LRECL'
020000       WHEN  104 DISPLAY 'INVALID RPL OPTIONS'
020100       WHEN  108 DISPLAY 'INVALID LRECL'
020200       WHEN  112 DISPLAY 'INVALID KEY LENGTH'
020300       WHEN  116 DISPLAY 'VIOLATED LOAD MODE RESTRICTION'
020400       WHEN  120 DISPLAY 'WRONG TASK SUBMITTING REQUEST'
020500       WHEN  132 DISPLAY 'TRYING TO GET SPANNED REC IN LOC MODE'
020600       WHEN  136 DISPLAY 'TRYING TO GET SPANNED REC BY ADDRESS'
020700                 DISPLAY 'IN KSDS'
020800       WHEN  140 DISPLAY 'INCONSISTENT SPANNED REC'
020900       WHEN  144 DISPLAY 'ALT INDEX POINTER WITH NO MATCHING'
021000                 DISPLAY 'BASE RECORD'
021100       WHEN  148 DISPLAY 'EXCEEDED MAX POINTERS IN ALT INDEX REC'
021200       WHEN  152 DISPLAY 'INSUFFICIENT BUFFERS AVAILABLE'
021300       WHEN  156 DISPLAY 'INVALID CONTROL INTERVAL'
021400       WHEN  192 DISPLAY 'INVALID RELATIVE REC NUMBER'
021500       WHEN  196 DISPLAY 'ATTEMPTED ADDRESSED REQUEST TO RRDS'
021600       WHEN  200 DISPLAY 'INVALID ACCESS THROUGH A PATH'
021700       WHEN  204 DISPLAY 'PUT IN BACKWARD MODE'
021800       WHEN  208 DISPLAY 'INVALID ENDREQ MACRO'
021900       WHEN OTHER DISPLAY 'UNKNOWN REASON'
022000     END-EVALUATE.
022100 ERROR-EXIT.
022200     CLOSE VSAM-KSDS-FILE
022300     GOBACK.
```

The JCL and data for VSAMSEQ2 are the same as for VSAMSEQ1. There is no need to compile and run VSAMSEQ2. It is for illustration purposes.

16. VSAMSEQ1, VSAMSEQ2. The VSAM File Read Sequentially

This page intentionally left blank

17. VSAMRND1. The VSAM KSDS, Read Randomly

VSAMRND1.

This program reads the same file as the previous program, VSAMSEQ1, but it reads it randomly. The program gives a key field (employee name in this case) to VSAM and says "get me the record with this key field." VSAM will find the record and give the entire record to your program, or perhaps it won't be able to find it and will give you a status code of 23 which means "not found." This program will just read two records, and the key field data will be hard coded - it will come from literals coded right in the program. This technique will keep the logic to a minimum and allow you to concentrate on the VSAM coding.

In the Real World, you will probably not be reading a VSAM file randomly based on hard coded information. However, this program will get you started reading VSAM randomly. It will come in handy in a real application, leading to effective VSAM coding.

The program **VSAMRND1:**

```
000100 IDENTIFICATION DIVISION.
000200 PROGRAM-ID. VSAMRND1.
000300* READ TWO VSAM KSDS RECORDS RANDOMLY
000400* BASED ON HARD CODED DATA
000500* JUST DISPLAY THE VSAM RECORDS
000600* NOTHING COMPLEX IN THIS PROGRAM
000700* THE LOGIC IS SIMPLE STRAIGHT LINE LOGIC
000800 ENVIRONMENT DIVISION.
000900 CONFIGURATION SECTION.
001000 INPUT-OUTPUT SECTION.
001100 FILE-CONTROL.
001200*    INPUT VSAM FILE IS: userid.VSAMKSDS.EMPSORTD
001300*
001500*    THE NAMES MAY BE DIFFERENT AT YOUR COMPANY
001600     SELECT VSAM-KSDS-FILE ASSIGN VSAMKSDS
001700        ORGANIZATION IS INDEXED
001800*     NOTICE THE RANDOM NEXT
001900        ACCESS MODE IS RANDOM
002000        RECORD KEY IS VSAM-KSDS-RECORD-KEY
000600        FILE STATUS  IS VSAM-STATUS-CODE
000700                        VSAM-EXTENDED-STATUS-CODE.
002200 DATA DIVISION.
002300 FILE SECTION.
002400
002500 FD  VSAM-KSDS-FILE.
002600 01  VSAM-KSDS-RECORD.
002700*    THE NEXT FIELD IN THIS PROGRAM IS THE RECORD KEY FIELD
002800*    THE KEY USED FOR SEARCHING IN THE FILE
002900*    YOU WILL BE MOVING A DATA VALUE TO THIS FIELD B4 THE READ
003000*    THE 20 MEANS THE KEY FIELD HAS A LENGTH OF 20
003100*    REFER  BACK TO THE JCL WHICH CREATES THE VSAM FILE
003200*    BECAUSE THAT IS WHERE THE 20 COMES FROM
003300*    THE RECORD KEY IS ACTUALLY EMPLOYEE NAME IN THIS DATA FILE
003400     05  VSAM-KSDS-RECORD-KEY    PIC X(20).
003500     05  VSAM-KSDS-EMP-INFO      PIC X(60).
```

17. VSAMRND1. The VSAM KSDS, Read Randomly

```
003700 WORKING-STORAGE SECTION.
001900 01  VSAM-STATUS-CODE.
002000     05 VSAM-STATUS-CODE-BYTE1    PIC X.
002100     05 VSAM-STATUS-CODE-BYTE2    PIC X.
002200
002300 01  VSAM-EXTENDED-STATUS-CODE.
002400     05 VSAM-EXTENDED-RETURN-CODE   PIC S9(4) COMP.
002500     05 VSAM-EXTENDED-FUNCTION-CODE PIC S9(4) COMP.
002600     05 VSAM-EXTENDED-FEEDBACK-CODE PIC S9(4) COMP.
004900
005000 PROCEDURE DIVISION.
005100     PERFORM INITIALIZATION
005200     PERFORM PROCESS-ALL
005300**    NOTICE NO UNTIL IN THIS PROGRAM
005400**    THIS PROGRAM WILL JUST BE READING 2 RECORDS
005500*        NO LOOP, NO UNTIL
005600     PERFORM TERMINATION
005700     GOBACK.
005800
005900 INITIALIZATION.
006000     OPEN INPUT VSAM-KSDS-FILE
006100     IF VSAM-STATUS-CODE IS NOT EQUAL TO '00'
006200     THEN GO TO ERROR-EXIT
006300     END-IF.
006400** NO NEED TO DO A READ HERE IN THIS PROGRAM
006500
006600 PROCESS-ALL.
006700*    THIS IS ALL THERE IS IN PROCESS-ALL PARAGRAPH IN THIS EXAMPLE
006800*    IT JUST READS 2 RECORDS RANDOMLY
006900     MOVE 'BUD WEIZER' TO VSAM-KSDS-RECORD-KEY
007000     PERFORM RANDOM-READ
007010 *    read record that is there
007020     Evaluate VSAM-STATUS-CODE
007030     WHEN '00' DISPLAY 'Found   ' VSAM-KSDS-RECORD-KEY
007040     WHEN '23' DISPLAY 'Not found' VSAM-KSDS-RECORD-KEY
007050     WHEN OTHER DISPLAY 'UNKNOWN REASON' VSAM-STATUS-CODE
007060          GO TO ERROR-EXIT
007070     END-EVALUATE.
007080 *    read record that is NOT there
007085     MOVE 'XXXXXXXXXX' TO VSAM-KSDS-RECORD-KEY
007090     PERFORM RANDOM-READ
007100
007110     Evaluate VSAM-STATUS-CODE
007120     WHEN '00' DISPLAY 'Found   ' VSAM-KSDS-RECORD-KEY
007130     WHEN '23' DISPLAY 'Not found' VSAM-KSDS-RECORD-KEY
007400     WHEN OTHER DISPLAY 'UNKNOWN REASON' VSAM-STATUS-CODE
007500          GO TO ERROR-EXIT
007600     END-EVALUATE.
008200
```

17. VSAMRND1. The VSAM KSDS, Read Randomly

```
008300 RANDOM-READ.
008400*     PLEASE NOTE THAT THERE IS NO AT END
008500*       (AT END IS FOR SEQUENTIAL READING ONLY, THIS IS RANDOM)
008600       READ VSAM-KSDS-FILE
008700       END-READ.
009000
009100 TERMINATION.
009200     CLOSE VSAM-KSDS-FILE.
009300
017400 ERROR-EXIT.
017500*   SEE THE PROGRAM VSAMSEQ2 FOR VSAM STATUS CODES
017510*   AND EXTENDED STATUS CODES
017520*   AND THE REMAINDER OF THIS PARAGRAPH
017530       Goback.
```

There is no need to create this dataset again. You created it for program VSAMSEQ1.
The data that you used as input to IDCAMS. IDCAMS created *userid*.VSAMKSDS.EMPSORTD
Before running IDCAMS, you uploaded the data and placed it in member
userid.COBBOOK.DATA(EMPSORTD)   The data is shown here for convenience.

```
          1         2         3         4         5         6
123456789.123456789.123456789.123456789.123456789.123456789.12345678

BUD WEIZER          05000 9 0001 0000001 000000
HERB GARDNER        03000 1 0040 0000055 000022
HUGH MUNGUS         06000 1 0200 0000020 000020
L. A. CALIFORNIA    07000 5 0020 0000033 000033
PAT SULLIVAN        04000 0 0002 0000022 000011
PEARLE E. GATES     01000 2 0010 0000020 000300
PHIL HARMONIC       02000 3 0030 0000050 000020
```

17. VSAMRND1. The VSAM KSDS, Read Randomly

Here is sample JCL:

The VSAM file was created for program VSAMSEQ1. There is no need to create it again.

```
//* vsamseq1/vsamrnd1.jcl
//DEFKSDS   EXEC PGM=IDCAMS
//SYSPRINT DD    SYSOUT=*
//SYSIN    DD    *
 DELETE (userid.VSAMKSDS.EMPSORTD) CLUSTER

 DEFINE CLUSTER -
 (NAME(userid.VSAMKSDS.EMPSORTD) -
  CYLINDERS(1,1) -
  KEYS(20,0) -
  RECORDSIZE(80,80) -
  VOLUMES(insert a volume serial number here) -
  INDEXED )

 REPRO INFILE(INFILE) OUTDATASET(userid.VSAMKSDS.EMPSORTD)

/*
//INFILE DD   DSN=userid.COBBOOK.DATA(EMPSORTD),DISP=SHR
//*
//STEP1    EXEC PGM=VSAMRND1
//STEPLIB DD DSN=your.executable.program.library.goes.here,DISP=SHR
//*  THE NEXT DATASET NAME MAY BE DIFFERENT AT YOUR COMPANY
//VSAMKSDS  DD   DSN=userid.VSAMKSDS.EMPSORTD,DISP=SHR
//SYSOUT    DD   SYSOUT=*
//SYSUDUMP  DD   SYSOUT=*
//SYSABOUT  DD   SYSOUT=*
//SYSDBOUT  DD   SYSOUT=*
//*
```

Expected results: (Displays are not formatted in any particular fashion.)
```
Found    BUD WEIZER
Not foundXXXXXXXXXX
```

18. VSAMRND2. The VSAM File, Read Randomly, Based on Records in a Regular Sequential File

VSAMRND2.

This is more Real World. There are at least two situations in which you might read a VSAM file randomly:

You are reading an ordinary sequential file in which the records are not in the same order as the VSAM file. You don't want to sort the sequential file, so you read them in the order they are in and then randomly read the corresponding record from the VSAM file. The model program VSAMRND2 works like this.

You have an on-line, interactive application. Data is keyed in at the terminal in no special order. You have to read the VSAM file randomly.

The program **VSAMRND2:**

```
000100 IDENTIFICATION DIVISION.
000200 PROGRAM-ID. VSAMRND2.
000300* READ VSAM KSDS RECORDS RANDOMLY
000400* BASED ON A REGULAR FILE READ SEQUENTIALLY
000500* JUST DISPLAY THE VSAM RECORDS
000600* NOTHING COMPLEX IN THIS PROGRAM
000700* THE LOGIC IS SAME AS REGULAR FILE READ SEQUENTIALLY
000800* IMPORTANT CLAUSES ARE   ORGANIZATION IS INDEXED
000900* ACCESS MODE IS RANDOM. OPEN INPUT
001000 ENVIRONMENT DIVISION.
001100 CONFIGURATION SECTION.
001200 INPUT-OUTPUT SECTION.
001300 FILE-CONTROL.
001400*     THIS IS AN ORDINARY SEQUENTIAL FILE: EMPNAMES
001500     SELECT IN-FILE   ASSIGN EMPNAMES.
001600*     INPUT VSAM FILE IS: userid.VSAMKSDS.EMPSORTD
001700*     USES EMPSORTD AS INPUT TO JCL
001800*      THE NAMES MAY BE DIFFERENT AT YOUR COMPANY
001900     SELECT VSAM-KSDS-FILE ASSIGN VSAMKSDS
002000        ORGANIZATION IS INDEXED
002100*     NOTICE THE RANDOM NEXT
002200        ACCESS MODE IS RANDOM
002300        RECORD KEY IS VSAM-KSDS-RECORD-KEY
002400        FILE STATUS   IS VSAM-STATUS-CODE
002500                        VSAM-EXTENDED-STATUS-CODE.
002600 DATA DIVISION.
002700 FILE SECTION.
002800 FD  IN-FILE
002900     RECORDING MODE IS F
003000     RECORD CONTAINS 80 CHARACTERS.
003100 01  IN-RECORD.
003200*     THE NEXT WILL BE USED AS THE KEY TO SEARCH IN THE VSAM FILE
003300*     IT HAS TO HAVE THE SAME PICTURE AS THE VSAM RECORD KEY
003400     05  EMPLOYEE-NAME          PIC X(20).
003500     05  FILLER                 PIC X(60).
003600
003700 FD  VSAM-KSDS-FILE
003800     RECORD CONTAINS 80 CHARACTERS.
003900 01  VSAM-KSDS-RECORD.
004000     05  VSAM-KSDS-RECORD-KEY   PIC X(20).
004100     05  VSAM-KSDS-EMP-INFO     PIC X(60).
```

18. VSAMRND2. The VSAM File, Read Randomly, Based on Records in a Regular Sequential File

```
004300 WORKING-STORAGE SECTION.
004400 01 SWITCHES.
004500     05  FILE-AT-END      PIC X  VALUE 'N'.
004600
004700 01  VSAM-STATUS-CODE.
004800     05 VSAM-STATUS-CODE-BYTE1    PIC X.
004900     05 VSAM-STATUS-CODE-BYTE2    PIC X.
005000
005100 01  VSAM-EXTENDED-STATUS-CODE.
005200     05 VSAM-EXTENDED-RETURN-CODE   PIC S9(4) COMP.
005300     05 VSAM-EXTENDED-FUNCTION-CODE PIC S9(4) COMP.
005400     05 VSAM-EXTENDED-FEEDBACK-CODE PIC S9(4) COMP.
005500
005600 PROCEDURE DIVISION.
005700     PERFORM INITIALIZATION
005800     PERFORM PROCESS-ALL
005900         UNTIL FILE-AT-END = 'Y'
006000     PERFORM TERMINATION
006100     GOBACK.
006200
006300 INITIALIZATION.
006400     OPEN INPUT IN-FILE
006500     OPEN INPUT VSAM-KSDS-FILE
006600     IF VSAM-STATUS-CODE IS NOT EQUAL TO '00'
006700     THEN GO TO ERROR-EXIT
006800     END-IF
006900     PERFORM READ-REGULAR-FILE.
007000
007100 PROCESS-ALL.
007200     PERFORM RANDOM-READ
007300     PERFORM READ-REGULAR-FILE.
007400
007500 TERMINATION.
007600     CLOSE IN-FILE VSAM-KSDS-FILE.
007700
007800 READ-REGULAR-FILE.
007900     READ IN-FILE
008000         AT END MOVE 'Y' TO FILE-AT-END
008100     END-READ.
```

18. VSAMRND2. The VSAM File, Read Randomly, Based on Records in a Regular Sequential File

```
008300 RANDOM-READ.
008400*    EMPLOYEE-NAME COMES FROM THE REGULAR INPUT FILE
008500*    IT MUST BE MOVED TO THE RECORD KEY OF THE VSAM FILE
008600*    THE RECORD KEY IS WHAT VSAM SEARCHES FOR IN THE FILE
008700*     IF IT FINDS IT, IT RETRIEVES THAT ENTIRE RECORD,
008800*     IF NOT, THEN STATUS CODE 23
008900     MOVE EMPLOYEE-NAME TO VSAM-KSDS-RECORD-KEY
009000     READ VSAM-KSDS-FILE
009100*    NOTE: THERE IS NO AT END
009200     END-READ
009400     EVALUATE VSAM-STATUS-CODE
009500        WHEN '23'
009600                DISPLAY 'NOT FOUND' EMPLOYEE-NAME
009700        WHEN '00'
009800*            ON A FOUND SITUATION IN REAL LIFE
009900*               YOU WOULD DO MORE THAN JUST DISPLAY THE RECORD
010000                DISPLAY 'FOUND' VSAM-KSDS-RECORD
010100        WHEN OTHER GO TO ERROR-EXIT
010200        END-EVALUATE.
010400 ERROR-EXIT.
010500*    SEE THE PROGRAM VSAMSEQ2 FOR VSAM STATUS CODES
010600*    AND EXTENDED STATUS CODES
010700*    AND THE REMAINDER OF THIS PARAGRAPH.
017530         Goback.
```

The input data file *userid*.**VSAMKSDS.EMPSORTD**: (the next two lines are a column ruler). It is input to the IDCAMS.

```
          1         2         3         4         5         6
123456789.123456789.123456789.123456789.123456789.123456789.12345678

BUD WEIZER            05000  9  0001  0000001  000000
HERB GARDNER          03000  1  0040  0000055  000022
HUGH MUNGUS           06000  1  0200  0000020  000020
L. A. CALIFORNIA      07000  5  0020  0000033  000033
PAT SULLIVAN          04000  0  0002  0000022  000011
PEARLE E. GATES       01000  2  0010  0000020  000300
PHIL HARMONIC         02000  3  0030  0000050  000020
```

The input data file **EMPNAMES**: (the next two lines are a column ruler)

```
          1         2         3         4         5         6
123456789.123456789.123456789.123456789.123456789.123456789.12345678

BUD WEIZER            YUP, HE S THERE
PHIL HARMONIC         OK
L. A. CALIFORNIA      OK TOO
HERB GARDNER          CALLING ALL GREEN THUMBS
HAL A. PENO           THIS ISN T THERE (TRY TACO BELL)
```

117

18. VSAMRND2. The VSAM File, Read Randomly, Based on Records in a Regular Sequential File

Here is sample JCL:
The VSAM file was created for program VSAMSEQ1. There is no need to create it again.

The VSAM file was created for program VSAMSEQ1. There is no need to create it again.

```
//* vsamseq1/vsamrnd1.jcl
//DEFKSDS  EXEC PGM=IDCAMS
//SYSPRINT DD   SYSOUT=*
//SYSIN    DD   *
 DELETE (userid.VSAMKSDS.EMPSORTD) CLUSTER

 DEFINE CLUSTER -
 (NAME(userid.VSAMKSDS.EMPSORTD) -
  CYLINDERS(1,1) -
  KEYS(20,0) -
  RECORDSIZE(80,80) -
  VOLUMES(insert a volume serial number here) -
  INDEXED )

 REPRO INFILE(INFILE) OUTDATASET(userid.VSAMKSDS.EMPSORTD)

/*
//INFILE DD   DSN=userid.COBBOOK.DATA(EMPSORTD),DISP=SHR
//*
//STEP1    EXEC PGM=VSAMRND2
//STEPLIB DD DSN=your.executable.program.library.here,DISP=SHR
//*  THE NEXT DATASET NAME MAY BE DIFFERENT AT YOUR CO
//VSAMKSDS   DD   DSN=userid.VSAMKSDS.EMPSORTD,DISP=SHR
//EMPNAMES   DD   DSN=userid.COBBOOK.DATA(EMPNAMES),DISP=SHR
//SYSOUT     DD   SYSOUT=*
//SYSUDUMP   DD   SYSOUT=*
//SYSABOUT   DD   SYSOUT=*
//SYSDBOUT   DD   SYSOUT=*
```

Expected output: (DISPLAYS are not formatted any particular way)

```
FOUNDBUD WEIZER          05000 9 0001 0000001 000000
FOUNDPHIL HARMONIC       02000 3 0030 0000050 000020
FOUNDL. A. CALIFORNIA    07000 5 0020 0000033 000033
FOUNDHERB GARDNER        03000 1 0040 0000055 000022
NOT FOUNDHAL A. PENO
```

19. VSAMLOD1. VSAM Initial Load

VSAMLOD1.

In this program you load a VSAM KSDS that has never contained data. This means that you just defined it, but never loaded it. You could have used the REPRO statement in the IDCAMS JCL to do the same thing. But if you do it yourself with COBOL coding you can validate the records, check the sequence, modify the records, reformat fields and anything else you need to do.

The program **VSAMLOD1:**

```
000100 IDENTIFICATION DIVISION.
000200 PROGRAM-ID. VSAMLOD1.
000300* INITIAL LOAD OF A VSAM FILE (FILE NEVER HAD RECORDS IN IT)
000400*   IMPLIED BY OPEN OUTPUT, ACCESS MODE SEQUENTIAL
000500*   AND WRITE
000600* BASED ON A REGULAR FILE READ SEQUENTIALLY
000700* THE LOGIC IS SAME AS REGULAR FILE READ SEQUENTIALLY
000710* IMPORTANT CLAUSES ARE
000720* ACCESS MODE IS SEQUENTIAL
000730* OPEN FOR OUTPUT
000740* STATUS CODE 21 IS OUT OF SEQUENCE
000800 ENVIRONMENT DIVISION.
000900 CONFIGURATION SECTION.
001000 INPUT-OUTPUT SECTION.
001100 FILE-CONTROL.
001200*    THIS IS AN ORDINARY SEQUENTIAL FILE: EMPSORTD
001300*    NEEDS TO BE IN SORTED ORDER, BY THE KEY (FIRST 20 CHARACTERS
001400     SELECT IN-FILE  ASSIGN EMPSORTD.
001500*    INPUT VSAM FILE IS: userid.VSAMKSDS.NOTLOADD.EMPSORTD
001600*     THE NAMES MAY BE DIFFERENT AT YOUR COMPANY
001700     SELECT VSAM-KSDS-FILE ASSIGN VSAMKSDS
001800        ORGANIZATION IS INDEXED
001900*    NOTICE THE SEQUENTIAL NEXT
002000        ACCESS MODE IS SEQUENTIAL
002100        RECORD KEY IS VSAM-KSDS-RECORD-KEY
000600        FILE STATUS  IS VSAM-STATUS-CODE
000700                        VSAM-EXTENDED-STATUS-CODE.
002300 DATA DIVISION.
002400 FILE SECTION.
002500 FD  IN-FILE
002600     RECORDING MODE IS F
003000     RECORD CONTAINS 80 CHARACTERS.
003010 01  IN-RECORD.
003020*    THE NEXT WILL BE USED AS THE KEY TO SEARCH IN THE VSAM FILE
003030*    IT HAS TO HAVE THE SAME PICTURE AS THE VSAM RECORD KEY
003040     05  EMPLOYEE-NAME          PIC X(20).
003050     05  EMPLOYEE-INFO          PIC X(60).
003200
003300 FD  VSAM-KSDS-FILE
003400     RECORD CONTAINS 80 CHARACTERS.
003500 01  VSAM-KSDS-RECORD.
003600     05  VSAM-KSDS-RECORD-KEY   PIC X(20).
003700     05  VSAM-KSDS-EMP-INFO     PIC X(60).
```

19. VSAMLOD1. VSAM Initial Load

```
003900 WORKING-STORAGE SECTION.
004000 01 SWITCHES.
004100      05  FILE-AT-END      PIC X  VALUE 'N'.
004200
001900 01  VSAM-STATUS-CODE.
002000      05 VSAM-STATUS-CODE-BYTE1    PIC X.
002100      05 VSAM-STATUS-CODE-BYTE2    PIC X.
002200
002300 01  VSAM-EXTENDED-STATUS-CODE.
002400      05 VSAM-EXTENDED-RETURN-CODE    PIC S9(4) COMP.
002500      05 VSAM-EXTENDED-FUNCTION-CODE PIC S9(4) COMP.
002600      05 VSAM-EXTENDED-FEEDBACK-CODE PIC S9(4) COMP.
005000
005700 PROCEDURE DIVISION.
005800      PERFORM INITIALIZATION
005900      PERFORM PROCESS-ALL
006000**       UPPER CASE Y
006100          UNTIL FILE-AT-END = 'Y'
006200      PERFORM TERMINATION
006300      GOBACK.
006400
006500 INITIALIZATION.
006600      OPEN INPUT IN-FILE
006700*     I PREFER A SEPARATE OPEN HERE FOR THE VSAM FILE
006800*      IT KEEPS THE TWO OPENS SEPARATE, AND KEEPS
006900*       ERROR SITUATIONS SEPARATE
007000*       OPEN OUTPUT FOR THE LOAD
007100*        OPEN EXTENDED FOR RESUMING AN INTERRUPTED LOAD
007200      OPEN OUTPUT VSAM-KSDS-FILE
007300      IF VSAM-STATUS-CODE IS NOT EQUAL TO '00'
007400      THEN GO TO ERROR-EXIT
007500      END-IF
007600      PERFORM READ-REGULAR-FILE.
007700
```

19. VSAMLOD1. VSAM Initial Load

```
007800 PROCESS-ALL.
007900*      THE FROM ON THE WRITE WILL MOVE THE FIELDS OF THE REGULAR RECORD
008000*       TO THE CORRESPONDING FIELDS OF THE VSAM FILE
008100      WRITE VSAM-KSDS-RECORD      FROM IN-RECORD
008200      EVALUATE VSAM-STATUS-CODE
008300        WHEN '21'
008400                  DISPLAY 'KEY OUT OF SEQUENCE ON LOAD'
008500                  EMPLOYEE-NAME
008600        WHEN '00'
008700                  DISPLAY 'ADDED OK' VSAM-KSDS-RECORD
008800        WHEN OTHER GO TO ERROR-EXIT
008900        END-EVALUATE.
009000      PERFORM READ-REGULAR-FILE.
009100
009200 TERMINATION.
009300      CLOSE IN-FILE VSAM-KSDS-FILE.
009400
009500 READ-REGULAR-FILE.
009600      READ IN-FILE
009700         AT END MOVE 'Y' TO FILE-AT-END
009800      END-READ.
009900
017400 ERROR-EXIT.
017500*    SEE THE PROGRAM VSAMSEQ2 FOR VSAM STATUS CODES
017510*    AND EXTENDED STATUS CODES
017520*    AND THE REMAINDER OF THIS PARAGRAPH
017540          Goback.
```

19. VSAMLOD1. VSAM Initial Load

The input data file **EMPSORTD**: (the next two lines are a column ruler)
It is input to VSAMLOD1.

```
         1         2         3         4         5         6
123456789.123456789.123456789.123456789.123456789.123456789.12345678

BUD WEIZER           05000 9 0001 0000001 000000
HERB GARDNER         03000 1 0040 0000055 000022
HUGH MUNGUS          06000 1 0200 0000020 000020
L. A. CALIFORNIA     07000 5 0020 0000033 000033
PAT SULLIVAN         04000 0 0002 0000022 000011
PEARLE E. GATES      01000 2 0010 0000020 000300
PHIL HARMONIC        02000 3 0030 0000050 000020
```

Here is sample JCL:
The VSAM file was created for program VSAMSEQ1. There is no need to create it again.

```
//* vsamlod1.jcl
//DEFKSDS   EXEC PGM=IDCAMS
//SYSPRINT DD    SYSOUT=*
//SYSIN     DD    *
 DELETE (userid.VSAMKSDS.NOTLOADD.EMPSORTD) CLUSTER

 DEFINE CLUSTER -
 (NAME(userid.VSAMKSDS.NOTLOADD.EMPSORTD) -
  CYLINDERS(1,1) -
  KEYS(20,0) -
  RECORDSIZE(80,80) -
  VOLUMES(insert a volume serial number here) -
  INDEXED )
/*
//*
//STEP1     EXEC PGM=VSAMLOD1
//STEPLIB DD DSN=your.executable.program.library.here,DISP=SHR
//*  THE NEXT DATASET NAME MAY BE DIFFERENT AT YOUR CO
//VSAMKSDS   DD    DSN=userid.VSAMKSDS.NOTLOADD.EMPSORTD,DISP=SHR
//EMPSORTD   DD    DSN=userid.COBBOOK.DATA(EMPSORTD),DISP=SHR
//SYSOUT     DD    SYSOUT=*
//SYSUDUMP   DD    SYSOUT=*
```

Expected output: (DISPLAYS are not formatted any particular way)

```
ADDED OKBUD WEIZER           05000 9 0001 0000001 000000
ADDED OKHERB GARDNER         03000 1 0040 0000055 000022
ADDED OKHUGH MUNGUS          06000 1 0200 0000020 000020
ADDED OKL. A. CALIFORNIA     07000 5 0020 0000033 000033
ADDED OKPAT SULLIVAN         04000 0 0002 0000022 000011
ADDED OKPEARLE E. GATES      01000 2 0010 0000020 000300
ADDED OKPHIL HARMONIC        02000 3 0030 0000050 000020
```

20. VSAMACD1. VSAM File Maintenance (Add, Change, Delete)

VSAMACD1.

This program will randomly add, change and delete records in a VSAM file. It reads a regular sequential file which contains transaction codes for Add, Change and Delete.

This type of file maintenance could be performed just as this program does, or it could be done based on data keyed in on an on line application.

The program **VSAMACD1:**

```
000100 IDENTIFICATION DIVISION.
000200 PROGRAM-ID. VSAMACD1.
000300* ADD, CHANGE OR DELETE VSAM RECORDS
000400* BASED ON TRANSACTION CODES IN A REGULAR FILE READ SEQUENTIALLY
000500* THE LOGIC IS BASED ON THAT OF THE REGULAR FILE READ SEQUENTIALL
000600* IMPORTANT CLAUSES ARE ORGANIZATION IS INDEXED
000700*     ACCESS MODE IS RANDOM OPEN I-O    USE WRITE TO ADD
000900*      CHANGE: DO READ (NO AT END) (23 IS NOT FOUND)
000910*             THEN REWRITE
000920*      ON DELETE, 23 IS NOT FOUND
001000 ENVIRONMENT DIVISION.
001100 CONFIGURATION SECTION.
001200 INPUT-OUTPUT SECTION.
001300 FILE-CONTROL.
001400*     THIS IS AN ORDINARY SEQUENTIAL FILE: EMPTRANS
001500      SELECT IN-FILE  ASSIGN EMPTRANS.
001600*    INPUT VSAM FILE IS: userid.VSAMKSDS.EMPSORTD
001700*    JCL TO CREATE INPUT FILE IS VSAMDEF
001800*    USES EMPSORTD AS INPUT TO JCL
001900*     THE NAMES MAY BE DIFFERENT AT YOUR COMPANY
002000      SELECT VSAM-KSDS-FILE ASSIGN VSAMKSDS
002100        ORGANIZATION IS INDEXED
002200*    NOTICE THE RANDOM NEXT
002300        ACCESS MODE IS RANDOM
002400        RECORD KEY IS VSAM-KSDS-RECORD-KEY
000600        FILE STATUS  IS VSAM-STATUS-CODE
000700                        VSAM-EXTENDED-STATUS-CODE.
002600 DATA DIVISION.
002700 FILE SECTION.
002800 FD  IN-FILE
002900     RECORDING MODE IS F
003200     RECORD CONTAINS 80 CHARACTERS.
003210 01  IN-RECORD.
003220     05  TRANS-CODE                 PIC X.
003230     05  FILLER                     PIC X(02).
003230*     THE NEXT WILL BE USED AS THE KEY TO SEARCH IN THE VSAM FILE
003240*     IT HAS TO HAVE THE SAME PICTURE AS THE VSAM RECORD KEY
003250     05  EMPLOYEE-NAME              PIC X(20).
003260     05  EMPLOYEE-INFO              PIC X(57).
003270
003280 FD  VSAM-KSDS-FILE.
003290 01  VSAM-KSDS-RECORD.
003300     05  VSAM-KSDS-RECORD-KEY   PIC X(20).
003310     05  VSAM-KSDS-EMP-INFO     PIC X(57).
003320     05  FILLER                 PIC X(03).
```

20. VSAMACD1. VSAM File Maintenance (Add, Change, Delete)

```
004000 WORKING-STORAGE SECTION.
004100 01 SWITCHES.
004200      05  FILE-AT-END     PIC X  VALUE 'N'.
001800
001900 01  VSAM-STATUS-CODE.
002000      05 VSAM-STATUS-CODE-BYTE1    PIC X.
002100      05 VSAM-STATUS-CODE-BYTE2    PIC X.
002200
002300 01  VSAM-EXTENDED-STATUS-CODE.
002400      05 VSAM-EXTENDED-RETURN-CODE    PIC S9(4) COMP.
002500      05 VSAM-EXTENDED-FUNCTION-CODE PIC S9(4) COMP.
002600      05 VSAM-EXTENDED-FEEDBACK-CODE PIC S9(4) COMP.
005300
006100 PROCEDURE DIVISION.
006200      PERFORM INITIALIZATION
006300      PERFORM PROCESS-ALL
006400          UNTIL FILE-AT-END = 'Y'
006500      PERFORM TERMINATION
006600      GOBACK.
006700
006800 INITIALIZATION.
006900      OPEN INPUT IN-FILE
007000*      NOTE THE OPEN I-O, THIS ALLOWS READ, WRITE, REWRITE, DELETE
007100      OPEN I-O VSAM-KSDS-FILE
007200      IF VSAM-STATUS-CODE IS NOT EQUAL TO '00'
007300      THEN GO TO ERROR-EXIT
007400      END-IF
007500      PERFORM READ-REGULAR-FILE.
007600
007700 PROCESS-ALL.
007800      PERFORM DO-MAINT
007900      PERFORM READ-REGULAR-FILE.
008000
008100 DO-MAINT.
008200      EVALUATE TRANS-CODE
008300        WHEN 'A' PERFORM ADD-TRANS
008400        WHEN 'C' PERFORM CHANGE-TRANS
008500        WHEN 'D' PERFORM DELETE-TRANS
008600        WHEN OTHER
008700             DISPLAY 'UNKNOWN TRANS CODE'
008800             DISPLAY IN-RECORD
008900       END-EVALUATE.
009000
009100 ADD-TRANS.
009200*     MOVE ALL FIELDS
009300      MOVE EMPLOYEE-NAME TO VSAM-KSDS-RECORD-KEY
009400      MOVE EMPLOYEE-INFO TO VSAM-KSDS-EMP-INFO
009500      WRITE VSAM-KSDS-RECORD
009600      EVALUATE VSAM-STATUS-CODE
009700       WHEN '22'
009800             DISPLAY 'DUPLICATE RECORD ON FILE'
009900             DISPLAY VSAM-KSDS-RECORD
010000       WHEN '00'
010100             DISPLAY 'ADDED - AOK '
010200             DISPLAY VSAM-KSDS-RECORD
010300       WHEN OTHER GO TO ERROR-EXIT
010400
010500       END-EVALUATE.
```

20. VSAMACD1. VSAM File Maintenance (Add, Change, Delete)

```
010700 CHANGE-TRANS.
010800*      MOVE KEY FIELD (DONE IN RANDOM-READ), READ THE RECORD
010900       PERFORM RANDOM-READ
011000       EVALUATE VSAM-STATUS-CODE
011100        WHEN '23'
011200             DISPLAY 'CANNOT CHANGE, NOT FOUND'
011300             VSAM-KSDS-RECORD
011400        WHEN '00'
011500             DISPLAY 'READ - AOK '
011600             DISPLAY VSAM-KSDS-RECORD
011700**        NOW DO THE ACTUAL UPDATE - NOTE REWRITE, NOT WRITE
011800             MOVE EMPLOYEE-INFO     TO VSAM-KSDS-EMP-INFO
011900             REWRITE VSAM-KSDS-RECORD
       *           SHOULD CHECK STATUS CODE FOR REWRITE HERE
012000        WHEN OTHER GO TO ERROR-EXIT
012100        END-EVALUATE.
012200
012400 DELETE-TRANS.
012500*      JUST MOVE THE KEY FIELD
012600       MOVE EMPLOYEE-NAME TO VSAM-KSDS-RECORD-KEY
012700       DELETE VSAM-KSDS-FILE
012800       EVALUATE VSAM-STATUS-CODE
012900        WHEN '23'
013000             DISPLAY 'CANNOT DELETE, NOT ON FILE'
013100             DISPLAY VSAM-KSDS-RECORD
013200         WHEN '00'
013300             DISPLAY 'DELETED - AOK '
013400             DISPLAY VSAM-KSDS-RECORD
013500        WHEN OTHER GO TO ERROR-EXIT
013600        END-EVALUATE.
013700
013800   TERMINATION.
013900      CLOSE IN-FILE VSAM-KSDS-FILE.
014000
014100 READ-REGULAR-FILE.
014200      READ IN-FILE
014300          AT END MOVE 'Y' TO FILE-AT-END
014400      END-READ.
014500
```

20. VSAMACD1. VSAM File Maintenance (Add, Change, Delete)

```
014600 RANDOM-READ.
014700*    EMPLOYEE-NAME COMES FROM THE REGULAR INPUT FILE
014800*    IT MUST BE MOVED TO THE RECORD KEY OF THE VSAM FILE
014900*    THE RECORD KEY IS WHAT VSAM SEARCHES FOR IN THE FILE
015000*     IF IT FINDS IT, IT RETRIEVES THAT ENTIRE RECORD,
015100*     IF NOT, THEN STATUS CODE 23
015200     MOVE EMPLOYEE-NAME TO VSAM-KSDS-RECORD-KEY
015300     READ VSAM-KSDS-FILE
015400*    NOTE: THERE IS NO AT END
015500     END-READ
015600
015700*    YOU DON'T HAVE TO DO THIS EVALUATE HERE, BECAUSE IT IS DONE
015800*     IN CHANGE-TRANS ABOVE. BUT LEAVE IT HERE ANYWAY.
015900     EVALUATE VSAM-STATUS-CODE
016000       WHEN '23'
016100              DISPLAY 'NOT FOUND' EMPLOYEE-NAME
016200       WHEN '00'
016300              DISPLAY 'FOUND    ' VSAM-KSDS-RECORD
016400       WHEN OTHER GO TO ERROR-EXIT
016500       END-EVALUATE.
016600
017400 ERROR-EXIT.
017500*    SEE THE PROGRAM VSAMSEQ2 FOR VSAM STATUS CODES
017510*    AND EXTENDED STATUS CODES
017520*    AND THE REMAINDER OF THIS PARAGRAPH
017540          Goback.
```

The input data file *userid*.**VSAMKSDS.EMPSORTD**: (the next two lines are a column ruler). It is input to IDCAMS.

```
         1         2         3         4         5         6
123456789.123456789.123456789.123456789.123456789.123456789.12345678

BUD WEIZER          05000  9  0001  0000001  000000
HERB GARDNER        03000  1  0040  0000055  000022
HUGH MUNGUS         06000  1  0200  0000020  000020
L. A. CALIFORNIA    07000  5  0020  0000033  000033
PAT SULLIVAN        04000  0  0002  0000022  000011
PEARLE E. GATES     01000  2  0010  0000020  000300
PHIL HARMONIC       02000  3  0030  0000050  000020
```

The input data file **EMPTRANS**: (the next two lines are a column ruler)

```
         1         2         3         4         5         6
123456789.123456789.123456789.123456789.123456789.123456789.12345678

A   ALLEN ROENTCH     05000  9  0001  0000001  000000
C   HERB GARDNER      03000  1  0040  0000055  000022
D   HUGH MUNGUS       06000  1  0200  0000020  000020
A   L. A. CALIFORNIA  07000  5  0020  0000033  000033
C   LISA CARR         04000  0  0002  0000022  000011
D   MAL A. MUTE       01000  2  0010  0000020  000300
X   PHIL HARMONIC     02000  3  0030  0000050  000020
```

20. VSAMACD1. VSAM File Maintenance (Add, Change, Delete)

Here is sample JCL:

The file *userid*.VSAMKSDS.EMPSORTD was created for the program VSAMSEQ1. There is no need to create it again.

```
//DEFKSDS  EXEC PGM=IDCAMS
//SYSPRINT DD   SYSOUT=*
//SYSIN    DD   *
 DELETE (userid.VSAMKSDS.EMPSORTD) CLUSTER

 DEFINE CLUSTER -
 (NAME(userid.VSAMKSDS.EMPSORTD) -
  CYLINDERS(1,1) -
  KEYS(20,0) -
  RECORDSIZE(80,80) -
  VOLUMES(insert a volume serial number here) -
  INDEXED )

 REPRO INFILE(INFILE) OUTDATASET(userid.VSAMKSDS.EMPSORTD)

/*
//INFILE DD   DSN=userid.COBBOOK.DATA(EMPSORTD),DISP=SHR
//*
//*
//STEP1    EXEC PGM=VSAMACD1
//STEPLIB DD DSN=your.executable.program.library..here,DISP=SHR
//*   THE NEXT DATASET NAME MAY BE DIFFERENT AT YOUR CO
//VSAMKSDS  DD   DSN=userid.VSAMKSDS.EMPSORTD,DISP=SHR
//EMPTRANS  DD   DSN=userid.COBBOOK.DATA(EMPTRANS),DISP=SHR
//SYSOUT    DD   SYSOUT=*
//SYSUDUMP  DD   SYSOUT=*
//SYSABOUT  DD   SYSOUT=*
//SYSDBOUT  DD   SYSOUT=*
//*
//PRINTVSM EXEC PGM=IDCAMS,COND=(0,LT)
//SYSPRINT DD   SYSOUT=*
//SYSIN    DD   *
 PRINT INDATASET(userid.VSAMKSDS.EMPSORTD) CHARACTER
/*
```

20. VSAMACD1. VSAM File Maintenance (Add, Change, Delete)

Expected output from program: (DISPLAYS are not formatted any particular way)

```
DUPLICATE RECORD ON FILE
ALLEN ROENTCH          05000  9  0001  0000001  000000
FOUND    HERB GARDNER        03000  1  0040  0000055  000022
READ - AOK
HERB GARDNER           03000  1  0040  0000055  000022
CANNOT DELETE, NOT ON FILE
HUGH MUNGUS            03000  1  0040  0000055  000022
DUPLICATE RECORD ON FILE
L. A. CALIFORNIA       07000  5  0020  0000033  000033
NOT FOUNDLISA CARR
CANNOT CHANGE, NOT FOUND
LISA CARR             07000  5  0020  0000033  000033
CANNOT DELETE, NOT ON FILE
MAL A. MUTE           07000  5  0020  0000033  000033
UNKNOWN TRANS CODE
X   PHIL HARMONIC        02000  3  0030  0000050  000020
```

Expected output from IDCAMS print step.
```
IDCAMS  SYSTEM SERVICES

  PRINT INDATASET(userid.VSAMKSDS.EMPSORTD) CHARACTER
IDCAMS  SYSTEM SERVICES
LISTING OF DATA SET -userid.VSAMKSDS.EMPSORTD
KEY OF RECORD - ALLEN ROENTCH
ALLEN ROENTCH          05000  9  0001  0000001  000000
KEY OF RECORD - BUD WEIZER
BUD WEIZER             05000  9  0001  0000001  000000
KEY OF RECORD - HERB GARDNER
HERB GARDNER           03000  1  0040  0000055  000022
KEY OF RECORD - L. A. CALIFORNIA
L. A. CALIFORNIA       07000  5  0020  0000033  000033
KEY OF RECORD - PAT SULLIVAN
PAT SULLIVAN           04000  0  0002  0000022  000011
KEY OF RECORD - PEARLE E. GATES
PEARLE E. GATES        01000  2  0010  0000020  000300
KEY OF RECORD - PHIL HARMONIC
PHIL HARMONIC          02000  3  0030  0000050  000020
IDC0005I NUMBER OF RECORDS PROCESSED WAS 7
IDC0001I FUNCTION COMPLETED, HIGHEST CONDITION CODE WAS 0
IDCAMS  SYSTEM SERVICES
```

21. VSAMSTR1. VSAM Read Sequentially, with START

VSAMSTR1.

We are going to read a VSAM file sequentially with a new twist: we will not start at the beginning of the VSAM file, we will start somewhere in the middle. It uses the START verb to start in the middle. Other than that, it is exactly like the VSAM KSDS read sequentially.

The program **VSAMSTR1:**

```
000100 IDENTIFICATION DIVISION.
000200 PROGRAM-ID. VSAMSTR1.
000300* READ VSAM KSDS SEQUENTIALLY
000400*           STARTING IN THE MIDDLE OF THE FILE: USES START
000500* JUST DISPLAY THE VSAM RECORDS
000600* THE LOGIC IS THE SAME AS FOR THE SIMPLE FILE READ SEQUENTIALLY
000700* IMPORTANT CLAUSES ARE ORGANIZATION IS INDEXED
000800* ACCESS MODE IS SEQUENTIAL    OPEN INPUT
000900* 23 ON A START IS CAN'T FIND, CAN'T DO IT. USE READ...AT END
001000 ENVIRONMENT DIVISION.
001100 CONFIGURATION SECTION.
001200 INPUT-OUTPUT SECTION.
001300 FILE-CONTROL.
001400*     INPUT VSAM FILE IS: userid.VSAMKSDS.EMPSORTD
001500*
001600*     USES EMPSORTD AS INPUT TO JCL
001700*      THE NAMES MAY BE DIFFERENT AT YOUR COMPANY
001800      SELECT VSAM-KSDS-FILE ASSIGN VSAMKSDS
001900         ORGANIZATION IS INDEXED
002000         ACCESS MODE IS SEQUENTIAL
002100         RECORD KEY IS VSAM-KSDS-RECORD-KEY
002200         FILE STATUS   IS VSAM-STATUS-CODE
002300                       VSAM-EXTENDED-STATUS-CODE.
002400 DATA DIVISION.
002500 FILE SECTION.
002700 FD  VSAM-KSDS-FILE.
002800 01  VSAM-KSDS-RECORD.
002900*    THE 20 MEANS THE KEY FIELD HAS A LENGTH OF 20
003000*    REFER  BACK TO THE JCL WHICH CREATES THE VSAM FILE
003100*    BECAUSE THAT IS WHERE THE 20 COMES FROM
003200*    THE RECORD KEY IS ACTUALLY EMPLOYEE NAME IN THIS DATA FILE
003300      05  VSAM-KSDS-RECORD-KEY    PIC X(20).
003400      05  VSAM-KSDS-EMP-INFO      PIC X(60).
003600 WORKING-STORAGE SECTION.
003700
003800 01  VSAM-STATUS-CODE.
003900      05 VSAM-STATUS-CODE-BYTE1    PIC X.
004000      05 VSAM-STATUS-CODE-BYTE2    PIC X.
004200 01  VSAM-EXTENDED-STATUS-CODE.
004300      05 VSAM-EXTENDED-RETURN-CODE   PIC S9(4) COMP.
004400      05 VSAM-EXTENDED-FUNCTION-CODE PIC S9(4) COMP.
004500      05 VSAM-EXTENDED-FEEDBACK-CODE PIC S9(4) COMP.
004600
004700 01  SWITCHES.
004800       05  FILE-AT-END      PIC X  VALUE 'N'.
```

21. VSAMSTR1. VSAM Read Sequentially, with START

```
005000 PROCEDURE DIVISION.
005100     PERFORM INITIALIZATION
005200     PERFORM PROCESS-ALL
005300         UNTIL FILE-AT-END = 'Y'
005400     PERFORM TERMINATION
005500     GOBACK.
005600
005700 INITIALIZATION.
005800     OPEN INPUT VSAM-KSDS-FILE
005900     IF VSAM-STATUS-CODE IS NOT EQUAL TO '00'
006000     THEN GO TO ERROR-EXIT
006100     END-IF
006200*      THIS IS WHAT IS ADDED, FOR THE START VERB
006300*      PLACE A DATA VALUE IN THE RECORD KEY
006400*      IT NEED NOT BE AN EXACT MATCH, IF YOU USE > (GREATER THAN)
006500     MOVE 'MAL A. MUTE' TO VSAM-KSDS-RECORD-KEY
006600     START VSAM-KSDS-FILE    KEY IS >  VSAM-KSDS-RECORD-KEY
006700     EVALUATE VSAM-STATUS-CODE
006800       WHEN '23'
006900*      YOU COULD TERMINATE THE PROGRAM HERE IF YOU WISH.
007000*       WE WILL KEEP GOING VALIANTLY
007100       DISPLAY 'CANNOT SUCCESSFULLY START'
007200       DISPLAY 'PROGRAM WILL START AT THE BEGINNING'
007300       DISPLAY 'AS IF START NOT DONE'
007400       WHEN '00'
007500                 DISPLAY 'START WAS SUCCESSFUL'
007600       WHEN OTHER GO TO ERROR-EXIT
007700       END-EVALUATE.
007800     PERFORM READ-PAR.
007900
008000 PROCESS-ALL.
008100*      THIS PROGRAM IS SIMPLE.
008200*      IT JUST DISPLAYS THE RECORDS OF THE VSAM FILE
008300*      OTHER PROGRAMS WOULD DO MORE INVOLVED PROCESSING
008400     DISPLAY VSAM-KSDS-RECORD
008500     PERFORM READ-PAR.
008600
008700 TERMINATION.
008800     CLOSE VSAM-KSDS-FILE.
008900
009000 READ-PAR.
009100     READ VSAM-KSDS-FILE
009200     AT END MOVE 'Y' TO FILE-AT-END
009300     NOT AT END
009400      IF VSAM-STATUS-CODE IS NOT EQUAL TO '00'
009500      THEN GO TO ERROR-EXIT
009600      END-IF
009700      END-READ.
009800
009900 ERROR-EXIT.
010000*    SEE THE PROGRAM VSAMSEQ2 FOR VSAM STATUS CODES
010100*    AND EXTENDED STATUS CODES
010200*    AND THE REMAINDER OF THIS PARAGRAPH
010300         Goback.
```

21. VSAMSTR1. VSAM Read Sequentially, with START

The input data file *userid*.**VSAMKSDS.EMPSORTD**: (the next two lines are a column ruler)

```
        1         2         3         4         5         6
123456789.123456789.123456789.123456789.123456789.123456789.12345678

BUD WEIZER            05000  9  0001  0000001  000000
HERB GARDNER         03000  1  0040  0000055  000022
HUGH MUNGUS          06000  1  0200  0000020  000020
L. A. CALIFORNIA     07000  5  0020  0000033  000033
PAT SULLIVAN         04000  0  0002  0000022  000011
PEARLE E. GATES      01000  2  0010  0000020  000300
PHIL HARMONIC        02000  3  0030  0000050  000020
```

Here is sample JCL: The file *userid*.VSAMKSDS.EMPSORTD was created for program VSAMSEQ1, and does not have to be created again.

```
//DEFKSDS   EXEC PGM=IDCAMS
//SYSPRINT DD    SYSOUT=*
//SYSIN     DD    *
 DELETE (userid.VSAMKSDS.EMPSORTD) CLUSTER

 DEFINE CLUSTER -
 (NAME(userid.VSAMKSDS.EMPSORTD) -
 CYLINDERS(1,1) -
 KEYS(20,0) -
 RECORDSIZE(80,80) -
 VOLUMES(insert a volume serial number here) -
 INDEXED )

 REPRO INFILE(INFILE) OUTDATASET(userid.VSAMKSDS.EMPSORTD)
/*
//INFILE DD   DSN=userid.COBBOOK.DATA(EMPSORTD),DISP=SHR
//*
//STEP1     EXEC PGM=VSAMSTR1
//STEPLIB DD DSN=your.executable.program.library.here,DISP=SHR
//*  THE NEXT DATASET NAME MAY BE DIFFERENT AT YOUR CO
//VSAMKSDS   DD   DSN=userid.VSAMKSDS.EMPSORTD,DISP=SHR
//SYSOUT    DD    SYSOUT=*
//SYSUDUMP  DD    SYSOUT=*
//SYSABOUT  DD    SYSOUT=*
//SYSDBOUT  DD    SYSOUT=*
```

Expected output from program: (DISPLAYS are not formatted any particular way)
```
START WAS SUCCESSFUL
PAT SULLIVAN         04000  0  0002  0000022  000011
PEARLE E. GATES      01000  2  0010  0000020  000300
PHIL HARMONIC        02000  3  0030  0000050  000020
```

21. VSAMSTR1. VSAM Read Sequentially, with START

This page intentionally left blank

22. VARWRIT1. Creating a Variable Format File

VARWRIT1.

This program creates a variable format file. The records in the file are of different lengths. This will save space on the disk or tape file where they are stored.

The secret to this is in the WRITE statement. To create a short record, you WRITE the short record. To create a medium, you WRITE the medium, etc.

If you simply send the output file to the printer, you won't know if you have actually created a variable format file. You must pass it to another program which will try to read it. We will do that with the JCL. So the JCL used with this program will not be shown until after the program that reads the file, VARREAD1. This will allow you to create both programs and then test them together in one set of JCL.

This set of two programs, VARWRIT1 and VARREAD1 doesn't do anything very complex. They simply create and use a variable format file. They will work properly only if you actually create a valid variable format file. Compile both before running the JCL.

The program **VARWRIT1**:

```
000200 IDENTIFICATION DIVISION.
000300 PROGRAM-ID. VARWRIT1.
000400* the input file is fixed format
000500* the output file is variable format
000600*     with three record lengths: 20, 40, 60
000700* this will create variable format records
000800* you won't be able to prove that they are really variable format
000900*    until you read the file with another program
001200 ENVIRONMENT DIVISION.
001300 CONFIGURATION SECTION.
001400 INPUT-OUTPUT SECTION.
001500 FILE-CONTROL.
001600*  INPUT FILE: fixedinp
001700     SELECT INFILE  ASSIGN FIXEDINP.
002100     SELECT OUTFILE ASSIGN VAROUT.
002500 DATA DIVISION.
002600 FILE SECTION.
002700 FD  INFILE
002810     RECORDING MODE IS F
003100     RECORD CONTAINS 80 CHARACTERS.
003110 01  IN-RECORD.
003120*    ALL RECORDS ARE SAME LENGTH - SO SPACE WASTED
003130     05  IN-RECORD-TYPE PIC X(09).
003140     05  IN-NAME-1      PIC X(10).
003150     05  IN-NAME-2      PIC X(10).
003160     05  IN-NAME-3      PIC X(10).
003170     05  IN-NAME-4      PIC X(10).
003180     05  IN-NAME-5      PIC X(10).
003190     05  FILLER         PIC X(21).
003200
```

22. VARWRIT1. Creating a Variable Format File

```
003400 FD   OUTFILE
003410      RECORDING MODE IS V
003600      RECORD CONTAINS 20 to 60 CHARACTERS.
003700*     MVS adds 4 to the maximum record length you put here
003800*     so 64 is really the maximum record length.
003900*     don't put  64 here, because MVS would make it 68...
004000*     if you use the LRECL parameter in JCL, it must be 64 , not
004100*     (the minimum record length means nothing -
004200*          you could put 0, 1, or 59...they all work the same)
004500*     note the three record descriptions.
004600*     the way you create a short record is to say
004700*      write short-record from ....
004800*     the way you create a medium record is to say
004900*      write medium-record from ....
005000*     the way you create a long record is to say
005100*      write long-record from ....
005200*       these can be in any order ....
005300 01   SHORT-RECORD  PIC X(20).
005400 01   MEDIUM-RECORD PIC X(40).
005500 01   LONG-RECORD   PIC X(60).
005600
005700 WORKING-STORAGE SECTION.
005800 01   SWITCHES.
005900      05   FILE-AT-END     PIC X  VALUE 'N'.
006000
006100*01  RECORD-COUNT            PIC S9(7) PACKED-DECIMAL VALUE +0.
006200*01  DISPLAY-RECORD-COUNT  PIC Z(6)9.
006300
007400 01   WS-SHORT-RECORD.
007500*     record is only 20 characters long
007600      05   SHORT-RECORD-TYPE PIC X(10).
007700      05   SHORT-NAME-1      PIC X(10).
007800*   no fillers needed
007900
008000 01   WS-MEDIUM-RECORD.
008100*     record is only 40 characters long
008200      05   MEDIUM-RECORD-TYPE PIC X(10).
008300      05   MEDIUM-NAME-1     PIC X(10).
008400      05   MEDIUM-NAME-2     PIC X(10).
008500      05   MEDIUM-NAME-3     PIC X(10).
008600*   no fillers needed
008700
008800 01   WS-LONG-RECORD.
008900**     record is only 60 characters long
009000      05   LONG-RECORD-TYPE PIC X(10).
009100      05   LONG-NAME-1 PIC X(10).
009200      05   LONG-NAME-2 PIC X(10).
009300      05   LONG-NAME-3 PIC X(10).
009400      05   LONG-NAME-4 PIC X(10).
009500      05   LONG-NAME-5 PIC X(10).
009600*   no fillers needed
009700
```

22. VARWRIT1. Creating a Variable Format File

```
009800 PROCEDURE DIVISION.
009900     PERFORM INITIALIZATION
010000     PERFORM PROCESS-ALL
010100**       UPPER CASE Y, PLEASE
010200         UNTIL FILE-AT-END = 'Y'
010300     PERFORM TERMINATION
010400     GOBACK.
010600 INITIALIZATION.
010700     OPEN INPUT  INFILE
010800          OUTPUT OUTFILE
010900     PERFORM READ-PAR.
011100 PROCESS-ALL.
011200*    don't really need to move spaces as in next line
011400     MOVE SPACES TO LONG-RECORD
011500     EVALUATE IN-RECORD-TYPE
011600     WHEN 'SHORT'  PERFORM WRITE-SHORT-RECORD
011700     WHEN 'MEDIUM' PERFORM WRITE-MEDIUM-RECORD
011800     WHEN 'LONG'   PERFORM WRITE-LONG-RECORD
011900     END-EVALUATE
012000
012100     PERFORM READ-PAR.
012200
012300 WRITE-SHORT-RECORD.
012400         MOVE IN-RECORD-TYPE TO SHORT-RECORD-TYPE
012500         MOVE IN-NAME-1 TO SHORT-NAME-1
012600         WRITE SHORT-RECORD FROM WS-SHORT-RECORD.
012700
012800 WRITE-MEDIUM-RECORD.
012900         MOVE IN-RECORD-TYPE TO MEDIUM-RECORD-TYPE
013000         MOVE IN-NAME-1 TO MEDIUM-NAME-1
013100         MOVE IN-NAME-2 TO MEDIUM-NAME-2
013200         MOVE IN-NAME-3 TO MEDIUM-NAME-3
013300         WRITE MEDIUM-RECORD FROM WS-MEDIUM-RECORD.
013400
013500 WRITE-LONG-RECORD.
013600         MOVE IN-RECORD-TYPE TO LONG-RECORD-TYPE
013700         MOVE IN-NAME-1 TO LONG-NAME-1
013800         MOVE IN-NAME-2 TO LONG-NAME-2
013900         MOVE IN-NAME-3 TO LONG-NAME-3
014000         MOVE IN-NAME-4 TO LONG-NAME-4
014100         MOVE IN-NAME-5 TO LONG-NAME-5
014200         WRITE LONG-RECORD FROM WS-LONG-RECORD.
014300
014400 TERMINATION.
014500     CLOSE INFILE OUTFILE.
014700 READ-PAR.
014800     READ INFILE
014900         AT END MOVE 'Y' TO FILE-AT-END
015000     END-READ.
```

Compile the program VARWRIT1. Do not run any JCL until after compiling VARREAD1.

22. VARWRIT1. Creating a Variable Format File

This page intentionally left blank

23. VARREAD1. Reading a Variable Format File

VARREAD1.

This program will read the variable format file created by the previous program, VARWRIT1. The secret to this is that you READ first, then check the record type field to see what kind of record you just got. Then move the record to the proper length working-storage data item.

The program **VARREAD1:**

```
000200 IDENTIFICATION DIVISION.
000300 PROGRAM-ID. VARREAD1.
000400* the input file is variable format
000500*    with three record lengths: 20, 40, 60
000600* you must read first,
000700* before you know if you have short, med, long
000900 ENVIRONMENT DIVISION.
001000 CONFIGURATION SECTION.
001100 INPUT-OUTPUT SECTION.
001200 FILE-CONTROL.
001300*  INPUT FILE: the one created by varwrit1 program
001400      SELECT INFILE   ASSIGN VARINP.
001800      SELECT OUTFILE ASSIGN REPORTFI.
002200 DATA DIVISION.
002300 FILE SECTION.
002500 FD  INFILE
002510      RECORDING MODE IS V
002700*    MVS adds 4 to the maximum record length you put here
002800*    so 64 is really the maximum record length.
002900*    don't put  64 here, because MVS would make it 68...
003000*    if you use the LRECL parameter in JCL, it must be 64 , not
003100*    (the minimum record length means nothing -
003200*        you could put 0, 1, or 59...they all work the same)
003300      RECORD CONTAINS 20 to 60 CHARACTERS.
003600*    note the three record descriptions.
003700*    you don't know which record type
003800*     you have read until you check the indicator
003900*        (the literal in the first 9 positions)
004000 01  WS-SHORT-RECORD.
004100*    record is only 20 characters long
004200      05   RECORD-TYPE  PIC X(10).
004300      05   SHORT-NAME-1 PIC X(10).
004400
004500 01  WS-MEDIUM-RECORD.
004600*    record is only 40 characters long
004700      05   filler       PIC X(10).
004800      05   MEDIUM-NAME-1 PIC X(10).
004900      05   MEDIUM-NAME-2 PIC X(10).
005000      05   MEDIUM-NAME-3 PIC X(10).
005100
005200 01  WS-LONG-RECORD.
005300**    record is only 60 characters long
005400      05   filler      PIC X(10).
005500      05   LONG-NAME-1 PIC X(10).
005600      05   LONG-NAME-2 PIC X(10).
005700      05   LONG-NAME-3 PIC X(10).
005800      05   LONG-NAME-4 PIC X(10).
005900      05   LONG-NAME-5 PIC X(10).
```

23. VARREAD1. Reading a Variable Format File

```
006100 FD  OUTFILE
006110     RECORDING MODE IS F
006400     RECORD CONTAINS 133 CHARACTERS.
006500 01  OUT-RECORD PIC X(133).
006600
006700 WORKING-STORAGE SECTION.
006800 01  SWITCHES.
006900     05  FILE-AT-END     PIC X  VALUE 'N'.
007000
007100 01  RECORD-COUNT         PIC S9(7) PACKED-DECIMAL VALUE +0.
007200 01  DISPLAY-RECORD-COUNT PIC Z(6)9.
007300
007400 01  WS-PRINT-LINE.
007500     05 FILLER        PIC X     VALUE SPACES.
007600     05 PRINT-NAME-1  PIC X(10) VALUE SPACES.
007700     05 FILLER        PIC X     VALUE SPACES.
007800     05 PRINT-NAME-2  PIC X(10) VALUE SPACES.
007900     05 FILLER        PIC X     VALUE SPACES.
008000     05 PRINT-NAME-3  PIC X(10) VALUE SPACES.
008100     05 FILLER        PIC X     VALUE SPACES.
008200     05 PRINT-NAME-4  PIC X(10) VALUE SPACES.
008300     05 FILLER        PIC X     VALUE SPACES.
008400     05 PRINT-NAME-5  PIC X(10) VALUE SPACES.
008500
008700 PROCEDURE DIVISION.
008800     PERFORM INITIALIZATION
008900     PERFORM PROCESS-ALL
009000**      UPPER CASE Y
009100       UNTIL FILE-AT-END = 'Y'
009200     PERFORM TERMINATION
009300     GOBACK.
009400
009500 INITIALIZATION.
009600     OPEN INPUT INFILE
009700          OUTPUT OUTFILE
009800     PERFORM READ-PAR.
009900
010000 PROCESS-ALL.
010100     EVALUATE RECORD-TYPE
010200       WHEN 'SHORT' PERFORM HAVE-SHORT-RECORD
010300       WHEN 'MEDIUM' PERFORM HAVE-MEDIUM-RECORD
010400       WHEN 'LONG' PERFORM HAVE-LONG-RECORD
010500       END-EVALUATE
010600
010700     PERFORM READ-PAR.
010800
010900 HAVE-SHORT-RECORD.
010950     DISPLAY 'HAVE SHORT   ' WS-SHORT-RECORD
011000     MOVE SPACES TO  WS-PRINT-LINE.
011100     MOVE SHORT-NAME-1 TO PRINT-NAME-1
011200     WRITE OUT-RECORD FROM WS-PRINT-LINE
011300           AFTER ADVANCING 1 LINE.
011400
```

23. VARREAD1. Reading a Variable Format File

```
011500 HAVE-MEDIUM-RECORD.
011550        DISPLAY 'HAVE MEDIUM  ' WS-MEDIUM-RECORD
011600        MOVE SPACES TO  WS-PRINT-LINE.
011700        MOVE MEDIUM-NAME-1 TO PRINT-NAME-1
011800        MOVE MEDIUM-NAME-2 TO PRINT-NAME-2
011900        MOVE MEDIUM-NAME-3 TO PRINT-NAME-3
012000        WRITE OUT-RECORD FROM WS-PRINT-LINE
012100              AFTER ADVANCING 1 LINE.
012200
012300 HAVE-LONG-RECORD.
012350        DISPLAY 'HAVE LONG    '   WS-LONG-RECORD
012400        MOVE SPACES TO  WS-PRINT-LINE.
012500        MOVE LONG-NAME-1 TO PRINT-NAME-1
012600        MOVE LONG-NAME-2 TO PRINT-NAME-2
012700        MOVE LONG-NAME-3 TO PRINT-NAME-3
012800        MOVE LONG-NAME-4 TO PRINT-NAME-4
012900        MOVE LONG-NAME-5 TO PRINT-NAME-5
013000        WRITE OUT-RECORD FROM WS-PRINT-LINE
013100              AFTER ADVANCING 1 LINE.
013200
013300 TERMINATION.
013400     CLOSE INFILE OUTFILE.
014001     DISPLAY 'VARREAD1 ENDING  '.
014010     MOVE RECORD-COUNT TO DISPLAY-RECORD-COUNT
014020     DISPLAY DISPLAY-RECORD-COUNT.
014500 READ-PAR.
015300     READ INFILE
015400         AT END MOVE 'Y' TO FILE-AT-END
015600     NOT AT END ADD 1 TO RECORD-COUNT
015700     END-READ.
```

23. VARREAD1. Reading a Variable Format File

The input data file **FIXEDINP**: (the next two lines are a column ruler)
It is input to the program VARWRIT1.

```
         1         2         3         4         5         6
123456789.123456789.123456789.123456789.123456789.123456789.12345678

MEDIUM     BETH       KELLY      ANTHONY
LONG       LAURA      RICK       NANCY      MARIA      ELLEN
SHORT      MOE
MEDIUM     NORMA      DENISE     JEAN
LONG       MAURA      NICK       SALLY      MARIO      ELLIE
```

Here is sample JCL that runs first program VARWRIT1 which passes its output file to program VARREAD1 which read it and verifies that it is OK:

```
//STEP1     EXEC PGM=VARWRIT1
//STEPLIB DD DSN=your.executable.program.library.here,DISP=SHR
//*   THE NEXT LIBRARY NAME MAY BE DIFFERENT AT YOUR CO
//FIXEDINP  DD    DSN=userid.COBBOOK.DATA(FIXEDINP),DISP=SHR
//VAROUT    DD    DSN=&&TEMPFILE,
//          DISP=(NEW,PASS),
//          UNIT=SYSDA,              MAY HAVE TO CHANGE SYSDA
//          SPACE=(TRK,(1)),
//          LRECL=64,RECFM=VB  64 is right - program's 60, +4
//SYSOUT    DD    SYSOUT=*
//SYSUDUMP  DD    SYSOUT=*
//*
//STEP2     EXEC PGM=VARREAD1
//STEPLIB DD DSN=your.executable.program.library.here,DISP=SHR
//*   THE NEXT LIBRARY NAME MAY BE DIFFERENT AT YOUR CO
//VARINP    DD    DSN=&&TEMPFILE,DISP=(OLD,DELETE),
//          LRECL=64,RECFM=VB
//REPORTFI  DD    SYSOUT=*
//SYSOUT    DD    SYSOUT=*
//SYSUDUMP  DD    SYSOUT=*
```

Expected output from VARREAD1: (DISPLAYS are not formatted any particular way)

```
have medium   MEDIUM     BETH       KELLY      ANTHONY
have long     LONG       LAURA      RICK       NANCY      MARIA      ELLEN
have short    SHORT      MOE
have medium   MEDIUM     NORMA      DENISE     JEAN
have long     LONG       MAURA      NICK       SALLY      MARIO      ELLIE
VARREAD1 ENDING
     5
```

24. VARODOW1. Creating a Variable Format File with Occurs Depending On

VARODOW1.

This program, VARODOW1 will create essentially the same file as the program VARWRIT1, but it will use an Occurs Depending On counter instead of the literals "SHORT", "MEDIUM" and "LONG" to show which type of record is being created. Otherwise, it will do the same thing as VARWRIT1.

Occurs Depending On involves data items whose length can actually change dynamically during the program's execution. The data item contains an Occurs clause, but the number of times it actually occurs is determined when the program is running.

Your Occurs clause in the program specifies a number, for example, ITEM-1 OCCURS 100 TIMES. This number is a MAXIMUM number of occurrences. Not to exceed this number! But it can occur fewer times, down to 0, that's zero occurrences (that means that the item occurs no times, so it has zero length, and has disappeared into the nearest space-warp.)

It gets better. Every time, during the program's execution, that you refer to the item with the Occurs Depending On, the COBOL compiler looks at the Occurs Depending On counter to see how many times it actually occurs. Then and only then does it know how many bytes it has to move or examine.

The main thing to remember is this: move a valid number to the Occurs Depending On counter BEFORE you refer in any way to the item. (When in doubt about what number to move to the Occurs Depending On counter, move the maximum number first, then the correct number later.) If you don't do it BEFORE, you may have an item of the wrong length. Not good. You may lose data or even worse, pick up data you didn't want.

Other than that, it's very simple.

You'll need to read this program's output file with the program VARODOR1, shown next. The JCL will be shown with the next program, VARODOR1.

24. VARODOW1. Creating a Variable Format File with Occurs Depending On

The program **VARODOW1:**

```
000200 IDENTIFICATION DIVISION.
000300 PROGRAM-ID. VARODOW1.
000400* the input file is fixed format
000500* the output file is variable format
000600*      with three record lengths: 20, 40, 60
000700* this will create variable format records
000800* using occurs depending on
001100*
001200 ENVIRONMENT DIVISION.
001300 CONFIGURATION SECTION.
001400 INPUT-OUTPUT SECTION.
001500 FILE-CONTROL.
001600      SELECT INFILE  ASSIGN FIXEDINP.
002000      SELECT OUTFILE ASSIGN VAROUT.
002400 DATA DIVISION.
002500 FILE SECTION.
002600 FD  INFILE
002610      RECORDING MODE IS F
003000      RECORD CONTAINS 80 CHARACTERS.
003100 01  IN-RECORD.
006100*     all records are same length - so space wasted
006200      05  IN-RECORD-TYPE PIC X(09).
006300      05  IN-NAME-1      PIC X(10).
006400      05  IN-NAME-2      PIC X(10).
006500      05  IN-NAME-3      PIC X(10).
006600      05  IN-NAME-4      PIC X(10).
006700      05  IN-NAME-5      PIC X(10).
006800      05  FILLER         PIC X(21).
003200
003300 FD  OUTFILE
003310      RECORDING MODE IS V
003500*     MVS adds 4 to the maximum record length you put here
003600*     so 64 is really the maximum record length.
003700*     don't put  64 here, because MVS would make it 68...
003800*     if you use the LRECL parameter in JCL, it must be 64 , not
003900*     (the minimum record length means nothing -
004000*          you could put 0, 1, or 59...they all work the same)
004100      RECORD CONTAINS 20 to 60 CHARACTERS.
004400
004500*     before actually writing out the record,
004600*     the compiler looks to see what the odo counter is
004700*     then calculates the length of out-record
004800*     then writes out only as many characters
004900*     as the length of the record
005000 01  OUT-RECORD.
005100      05 ODO-COUNTER  PIC 9(5) VALUE 5.
005200      05 FILLER       PIC X(5) VALUE SPACES.
005300      05 OUTPUT-NAME  PIC X(10)
005400         OCCURS 5 TIMES DEPENDING ON ODO-COUNTER.
005500
```

24. VARODOW1. Creating a Variable Format File with Occurs Depending On

```
005600 WORKING-STORAGE SECTION.
005700 01   SWITCHES.
005800      05  FILE-AT-END      PIC X   VALUE 'N'.
005900
007000 01  WS-short-RECORD.
007100*     record is only 20 characters long
007200      05   SHORT-RECORD-TYPE PIC X(10).
007300      05   SHORT-NAME-1      PIC X(10).
007400*   that's all, no fillers
007500
007600 01   WS-medium-RECORD.
007700*     record is only 40 characters long
007800      05   MEDIUM-RECORD-TYPE PIC X(10).
007900      05   MEDIUM-NAME-1      PIC X(10).
008000      05   MEDIUM-NAME-2      PIC X(10).
008100      05   MEDIUM-NAME-3      PIC X(10).
008200*   that's all, no fillers
008300
008400 01   WS-long-RECORD.
008500**      record is only 60 characters long
008600      05   LONG-RECORD-TYPE PIC X(10).
008700      05   LONG-NAME-1       PIC X(10).
008800      05   LONG-NAME-2       PIC X(10).
008900      05   LONG-NAME-3       PIC X(10).
009000      05   LONG-NAME-4       PIC X(10).
009100      05   LONG-NAME-5       PIC X(10).
009200*   that's all, no fillers
009300
009400 PROCEDURE DIVISION.
009500      PERFORM INITIALIZATION
009600      PERFORM PROCESS-ALL
009700**       UPPER CASE Y
009800         UNTIL FILE-AT-END = 'Y'
009900      PERFORM TERMINATION
010000      GOBACK.
010100
```

24. VARODOW1. Creating a Variable Format File with Occurs Depending On

```
010200 INITIALIZATION.
010300     OPEN INPUT INFILE
010400          OUTPUT OUTFILE
010500     PERFORM READ-PAR.
010600
010700 PROCESS-ALL.
010800*    don't really need to move spaces as in next line
011000     MOVE SPACES TO OUT-RECORD
011100     EVALUATE IN-RECORD-TYPE
011200      WHEN 'SHORT'  PERFORM WRITE-SHORT-RECORD
011300      WHEN 'MEDIUM' PERFORM WRITE-MEDIUM-RECORD
011400      WHEN 'LONG'   PERFORM WRITE-LONG-RECORD
011500     END-EVALUATE
011600
011700     PERFORM READ-PAR.
011800
011900 WRITE-SHORT-RECORD.
012000*       there are other more sophisticated
012100*       ways to do it, but I'm trying to keep it simple
012200*       be sure to move the number to the counter first
012300       MOVE 1 TO ODO-COUNTER
012400       MOVE IN-NAME-1 TO OUTPUT-NAME (1)
012500*      let's not do a write FROM
012600*      because this way is simpler
012700*      if you wrote FROM something, that thing
012800*      would need its own odo counter, so more complexity
012900       WRITE OUT-RECORD.
013000
013100 WRITE-MEDIUM-RECORD.
013200*       be sure to move the number to the counter first
013300       MOVE 3 TO ODO-COUNTER
013400       MOVE IN-NAME-1 TO OUTPUT-NAME (1)
013500       MOVE IN-NAME-2 TO OUTPUT-NAME (2)
013600       MOVE IN-NAME-3 TO OUTPUT-NAME (3)
013700       WRITE OUT-RECORD.
013800
013900 WRITE-LONG-RECORD.
014000*       be sure to move the number to the counter first
014100       MOVE 5 TO ODO-COUNTER
014200       MOVE IN-NAME-1 TO OUTPUT-NAME (1)
014300       MOVE IN-NAME-2 TO OUTPUT-NAME (2)
014400       MOVE IN-NAME-3 TO OUTPUT-NAME (3)
014500       MOVE IN-NAME-4 TO OUTPUT-NAME (4)
014600       MOVE IN-NAME-5 TO OUTPUT-NAME (5)
014700       WRITE OUT-RECORD.
014900 TERMINATION.
015000     CLOSE INFILE OUTFILE.
015100
015200 READ-PAR.
015300     READ INFILE
015400          AT END MOVE 'Y' TO FILE-AT-END
015500     END-READ.
```

Compile this program. You can run it after compiling the next program, VARODOR1

24. VARODOW1. Creating a Variable Format File with Occurs Depending On

The input data file **FIXEDINP**: (the next two lines are a column ruler)

```
         1         2         3         4         5         6
123456789.123456789.123456789.123456789.123456789.123456789.12345678

MEDIUM    BETH      KELLY     ANTHONY
LONG      LAURA     RICK      NANCY     MARIA     ELLEN
SHORT     MOE
MEDIUM    NORMA     DENISE    JEAN
LONG      MAURA     NICK      SALLY     MARIO     ELLIE
```

24. VARODOW1. Creating a Variable Format File with Occurs Depending On

This page intentionally left blank

25. VARODOR1. Reading a Variable Format File with Occurs Depending On

VARODOR1.

This program, VARODOR1 will read the variable format data file created by VARODOW1. Notice how easy it is to read this file: the program's logic is very simple. The Occurs Depending On handles the record length automatically.

The program **VARODOR1:**

```
000200 IDENTIFICATION DIVISION.
000300 PROGRAM-ID. VARODOR1.
000400* the input file is variable format
000500*    with three record lengths: 20, 40, 60
000600* the occurs depending on counter
000700* tells if you have short, med, long
000800*
000900 ENVIRONMENT DIVISION.
001000 CONFIGURATION SECTION.
001100 INPUT-OUTPUT SECTION.
001200 FILE-CONTROL.
001300*  INPUT FILE: is from program varodow1
001400     SELECT INFILE  ASSIGN INFILE.
001800     SELECT OUTFILE ASSIGN REPORTFI.
002200 DATA DIVISION.
002300 FILE SECTION.
002400
002500 FD  INFILE
002510     RECORDING MODE IS V
002800*     so 64 is really the maximum record length.
002900*     don't put  64 here, because MVS would make it 68...
003000*     if you use the LRECL parameter in JCL, it must be 64 , not
003100*     (the minimum record length means nothing -
003200*          you could put 0, 1, or 59...they all work the same)
003300     RECORD CONTAINS 20 to 60 CHARACTERS.
003600*     this record description is the same as
003700*     the one used for creating it - see program varodow1
003800 01  IN-RECORD.
003900     05 ODO-COUNTER PIC 9(5).
004000     05 FILLER      PIC X(5).
004100     05 INPUT-NAME  PIC X(10)
004200        OCCURS 5 TIMES DEPENDING ON ODO-COUNTER.
004300
004400 FD  OUTFILE
004410     RECORDING MODE IS F
004800     RECORD CONTAINS 133 CHARACTERS.
004900 01  OUT-RECORD PIC X(133).
005000
005100 WORKING-STORAGE SECTION.
005200 01  SWITCHES.
005300     05  FILE-AT-END      PIC X   VALUE 'N'.
005400
005500 01  WS-PRINT-LINE.
005600     05 FILLER            PIC X VALUE SPACE.
005700     05 WS-PRINT-LINE-DATA PIC X(132) VALUE SPACES.
005800
```

25. VARODOR1. Reading a Variable Format File with Occurs Depending On

```
005900 PROCEDURE DIVISION.
006000     PERFORM INITIALIZATION
006100     PERFORM PROCESS-ALL
006200**       upper case Y
006300            UNTIL FILE-AT-END = 'Y'
006400     PERFORM TERMINATION
006500     GOBACK.
006600
006700 INITIALIZATION.
006800     OPEN INPUT INFILE
006900          OUTPUT OUTFILE
007000     PERFORM READ-PAR.
007100
007200 PROCESS-ALL.
007300        MOVE SPACES TO  WS-PRINT-LINE.
007400*    this next move will move only as much
007500*    of in-record as needed
007600*    it looks at the odo counter first
007700*    to determine how long in-record is
007800     MOVE IN-RECORD TO WS-PRINT-LINE-DATA
007900     WRITE OUT-RECORD FROM WS-PRINT-LINE-DATA
008000          AFTER ADVANCING 1 LINE
008100     PERFORM READ-PAR.
008200
008300 TERMINATION.
008400     CLOSE INFILE OUTFILE.
008500
008600 READ-PAR.
008700*    we are not reading INTO here
008800*    because we don't know what to read into
008900*    until we have already read a record
009000     READ INFILE
009100         AT END MOVE 'Y' TO FILE-AT-END
009200     END-READ.
```

25. VARODOR1. Reading a Variable Format File with Occurs Depending On

Here is sample JCL:

(VARODOW1 is from the previous chapter. It should have been compiled already.)

```
//STEP1      EXEC PGM=VARODOW1
//STEPLIB DD DSN=your.executable.program.library.here,DISP=SHR
//*   THE NEXT LIBRARY NAME MAY BE DIFFERENT AT YOUR CO
//FIXEDINP  DD    DSN=userid.COBBOOK.DATA(FIXEDINP),DISP=SHR
//VAROUT    DD    DSN=&&TEMPFILE,
//                DISP=(NEW,PASS),
//                UNIT=SYSDA,              MAY HAVE TO CHANGE SYSDA
//                SPACE=(TRK,(1)),
//                LRECL=64,RECFM=VB  64 IS RIGHT PROGRAM SAYS 60, +4
//SYSOUT    DD    SYSOUT=*
//SYSUDUMP  DD    SYSOUT=*
//*
//STEP2      EXEC PGM=VARODOR1
//STEPLIB DD DSN=your.executable.program.library.here,DISP=SHR
//*   THE NEXT LIBRARY NAME MAY BE DIFFERENT AT YOUR CO
//INFILE    DD    DSN=&&TEMPFILE,DISP=(OLD,DELETE),
//                LRECL=64,RECFM=VB
//REPORTFI  DD    SYSOUT=*
//SYSOUT    DD    SYSOUT=*
//SYSUDUMP  DD    SYSOUT=*
```

Expected output after running VARODOW1 and VARODOR1.

```
00003     BETH      KELLY     ANTHONY
00005     LAURA     RICK      NANCY     MARIA     ELLEN
00001     MOE
00003     NORMA     DENISE    JEAN
00005     MAURA     NICK      SALLY     MARIO     ELLIE
```

25. VARODOR1. Reading a Variable Format File with Occurs Depending On

This page intentionally left blank

26. LOADODO1. The Table Load with Occurs Depending On

LOADODO1.

The table load program LOADTBL2 works very well, but has a problem. It wastes time. This is because the table in LOADTBL2 always occurs the maximum number of times, 100 in this example. Every time you do a SEARCH, it assumes that there are 100 occurrences (which there are!) and searches through empty occurrences. In order to get usable results with LOADTBL2 we had to place high-values in the empty occurrences. Not too swift.

Occurs Depending On to the rescue! By using this facility we can shorten the search time, since the empty occurrences will not be there - the Occurs Depending On will make them vanish! As with everything concerning Occurs Depending On, be careful. You must move a valid number to the Occurs Depending On counter before you use the data item.

In this program the table will occur only as many times as there are entries in the table. This will make the SEARCH verb sharply cut back its search: it will search only the occurrences that have something in them. Because of that we don't need to put high-values in the unused entries in the table.

The program **LOADODO1**:

```
000200 IDENTIFICATION DIVISION.
000300 PROGRAM-ID. LOADODO1.
000400* Load a table from a sequential file
000500* read a regular file
000600* check each record to see if it has a valid part number
000700* uses occurs depending on to shorten the length of the table
000800* there are only two differences between this and LOADTBL2
000900*     the occurs depending on clause in the table
001000*     and the set PART-TABLE-MAX-OCCURS
001100*     to the index, in the table-termination paragraph
001200*
001300 ENVIRONMENT DIVISION.
001400 CONFIGURATION SECTION.
001500 INPUT-OUTPUT SECTION.
001600 FILE-CONTROL.
001700*    TABLE FILE PARTTABL
001800     SELECT TABLE-FILE  ASSIGN PARTTABL.
002200*    REGULAR INPUT FILE PARTS1
002300     SELECT INFILE      ASSIGN PARTS1.
002700  DATA DIVISION.
002800 FILE SECTION.
002900 FD  TABLE-FILE
002910     RECORDING MODE IS F
003300     RECORD CONTAINS 80 CHARACTERS.
003400 01  TABLE-RECORD.
003410     05  WS-TR-PART-NUMBER      PIC X(6).
003420     05  WS-TR-PART-DESC        PIC X(30).
003440     05  FILLER                 PIC X(44).
003500
```

26. LOADODO1. The Table Load with Occurs Depending On

```
003600 FD  INFILE
003610     RECORDING MODE IS F
004000     RECORD CONTAINS 80 CHARACTERS.
004100 01  INFILE-RECORD.
004110*     PICTURES MUST CORRESPOND TO THE ACTUAL INPUT FILE
004120     05  PART-NUMBER           PIC X(6).
004130     05  PART-DESCR            PIC X(30).
004140     05  QTY-ON-HAND           PIC 9(3).
004150     05  QTY-ON-ORDER          PIC 9(3).
004160     05  QTY-ON-RESERVE        PIC 9(3).
004170     05  PART-PRICE            PIC 9(3)V99.
004180     05  UNUSED                PIC X(30).
004190
004300 WORKING-STORAGE SECTION.
004400 01  SWITCHES.
004500     05  TABLE-FILE-AT-END     PIC X  VALUE 'N'.
004600     05  INFILE-AT-END         PIC X  VALUE 'N'.
004700     05  VALID-SW              PIC X  VALUE 'Y'.
004800     05  SOMETHING-ON-TABLE    PIC X  VALUE 'N'.
004810     05  TABLE-OVERFLOW        PIC X  VALUE 'N'.
006500 01  PART-TABLE.
006600*    The 10 used here is arbitrary.
006700*    use whatever number you need for the size of your table
006800     05  EACH-PART-INFO     OCCURS 10 TIMES
006900         DEPENDING ON PART-TABLE-MAX-LOADED
007100         ASCENDING KEY IS EACH-PART-NUMBER
007110         INDEXED BY PART-INDEX.
007200         10 EACH-PART-NUMBER      PIC X(6).
007300         10 EACH-PART-DESCRIPTION PIC X(30).
007400*    The value of the next item must be the same as the occurs
007450 01  PART-TABLE-MAX-OCCURS pic S9(5) BINARY VALUE +10

007500*     notice: the next item
007600*     after loading the table - will contain the number
007700*     of actual entries you placed in the table
     *      however, initialize it the same as the previous
007800 01  PART-TABLE-MAX-LOADED pic S9(5) BINARY VALUE +10.
007900
008000 PROCEDURE DIVISION.
008100     PERFORM TABLE-INITIALIZATION
008200     PERFORM TABLE-PROCESS-ALL
008300         UNTIL TABLE-FILE-AT-END = 'Y'
008600     PERFORM TABLE-TERMINATION
008700*      from now on, part-table-max-loaded contains
008800**     the actual number of occurences
008900     PERFORM INFILE-INITIALIZATION
009000     PERFORM INFILE-PROCESS-ALL
009100         UNTIL INFILE-AT-END = 'Y'
009200     PERFORM INFILE-TERMINATION
009300     GOBACK.
009400
```

26. LOADODO1. The Table Load with Occurs Depending On

```
009500 TABLE-INITIALIZATION.
009600*     don't need to move high-values to part-table
009700*     Absolutely must set the index to 1
009800*     an index does not have a default initial value
009900*     and you are not allowed to set an index to 0
010000      SET PART-INDEX TO 1
010100      OPEN INPUT TABLE-FILE
010200      PERFORM TABLE-READ-PAR.
010300
010400 TABLE-PROCESS-ALL.
006110      IF PART-INDEX > PART-TABLE-MAX-OCCURS
006120      THEN
006130         MOVE 'Y' TO TABLE-FILE-AT-END
006140         MOVE 'Y' TO TABLE-OVERFLOW
006150            DISPLAY 'INDEX GT MAX'
006160      ELSE
006170         MOVE TABLE-RECORD TO EACH-PART-INFO(PART-INDEX)
006180         MOVE 'Y' TO SOMETHING-IN-TABLE
006190         SET PART-INDEX UP BY 1
006191         SET part-table-max-loaded to PART-INDEX
006192         PERFORM TABLE-READ-PAR
006193      END-IF.
010900
011000 TABLE-TERMINATION.
006700*     AT THIS POINT CHECK TO SEE IF THE TABLE
006800*     WAS PROPERLY LOADED
006910      IF TABLE-OVERFLOW = 'Y'
006920      THEN
006930         DISPLAY 'MORE RECORDS THAN TABLE ENTRIES'
006940         GO TO ERROR-EXIT
006950      END-IF
006960
006970      IF SOMETHING-IN-TABLE = 'Y'
006980      THEN
006990         DISPLAY 'TABLE APPEARS TO BE LOADED OK'
006991      ELSE
006992         DISPLAY 'NOTHING LOADED IN TABLE'
006993         GO TO ERROR-EXIT
006994      END-IF
006995
006996*     DISPLAY 'loaded ' part-table-max-loaded
006997
006998*     Next part is optional   commenting it out for now
006999*     IT DISPLAYS ALL THE ENTRIES IN THE TABLE - JUST TO SHOW
007000*     IF IT WORKED PROPERLY
007001*     DISPLAY 'THE TABLE AFTER LOADING'
007002*     PERFORM
007003*        VARYING PART-INDEX FROM 1 BY 1
007004*        UNTIL   PART-INDEX > PART-TABLE-MAX-OCCURS
007005*
007006*        DISPLAY EACH-PART-NUMBER (PART-INDEX)
007007*                EACH-PART-DESCRIPTION (PART-INDEX)
007008*     END-PERFORM
007009
007800      CLOSE TABLE-FILE.
```

26. LOADODO1. The Table Load with Occurs Depending On

```
013100
013200 TABLE-READ-PAR.
013300     READ TABLE-FILE
013400        AT END MOVE 'Y' TO TABLE-FILE-AT-END
013500     END-READ.
013600
013700 INFILE-INITIALIZATION.
013800     OPEN INPUT INFILE
013900     PERFORM INFILE-READ-PAR.
014000
014100 INFILE-PROCESS-ALL.
014200     MOVE 'Y' TO VALID-SW
014300     PERFORM TABLE-LOOKUP
014400     IF VALID-SW = 'Y'
014500*        Not doing much of anything here in this program
014600*        but you could write out records,
014700*        print lines in report, etc
014800        DISPLAY 'GOOD RECORD' INFILE-RECORD
014900     ELSE
015000        DISPLAY 'BAD RECORD' INFILE-RECORD
015100     END-IF
015200     PERFORM INFILE-READ-PAR.
015300
015400 INFILE-TERMINATION.
015500     CLOSE INFILE.
015700 INFILE-READ-PAR.
015800     READ INFILE
015900        AT END MOVE 'Y' TO INFILE-AT-END
016000     END-READ.
016200 TABLE-LOOKUP.
016300* This is a binary search
016400
016500        SEARCH ALL EACH-PART-INFO
016600        AT END
016700*        DISPLAY 'NOT FOUND'
016800        MOVE 'N' TO VALID-SW
016900        WHEN EACH-PART-NUMBER(PART-INDEX) = PART-NUMBER
017000*        DISPLAY 'FOUND'
017100        MOVE EACH-PART-DESCRIPTION(PART-INDEX) TO PART-DESCR
017200        MOVE 'Y' TO VALID-SW
017300        END-SEARCH.
017400
017500 ERROR-EXIT.
017600     DISPLAY 'PROGRAM IS BEING TERMINATED'
017700     DISPLAY 'PROBLEM WITH LOADING TABLE'
017800     GOBACK.
```

26. LOADODO1. The Table Load with Occurs Depending On

The input data file **PARTTABL**: (the next two lines are a column ruler)

```
         1         2         3         4         5         6
123456789.123456789.123456789.123456789.123456789.123456789.12345678

PART01 LEFT HANDED WIDGET WRENCHES     003 007 002 10022
PART02 LEAD-WINGED GLIDERS             004 006 001 14054
PART04 LEFT FOOT REEBOKS               021 002 004 04323
PART06 286 COMPUTERS W 4K HARD DISK    043 077 012 00042
```

The input data file **PARTS1**: (the next two lines are a column ruler)

```
         1         2         3         4         5         6
123456789.123456789.123456789.123456789.123456789.123456789.12345678

PART01                                 003 007 002 10022
PART02                                 004 006 001 14054
PART04                                 021 002 004 04323
PART06                                 043 077 012 00042
```

26. LOADODO1. The Table Load with Occurs Depending On

Here is sample JCL:

```
//STEP1     EXEC PGM=LOADODO1
//STEPLIB DD DSN=your.executable.program.library.here,DISP=SHR
//*   THE NEXT LIBRARY NAME MAY BE DIFFERENT AT YOUR CO
//PARTTABL   DD    DSN=userid.COBBOOK.DATA(PARTTABL),DISP=SHR
//PARTS1     DD    DSN=userid.COBBOOK.DATA(PARTS1),DISP=SHR
//SYSOUT     DD    SYSOUT=*
//SYSUDUMP   DD    SYSOUT=*
```

Expected output: (DISPLAYS are not formatted any particular way)

```
TABLE APPEARS TO BE LOADED OK
PART01found
GOOD RECORDPART01 LEFT HANDED WIDGET WRENCHES    003 007 002 10022
PART02found
GOOD RECORDPART02 LEAD-WINGED GLIDERS           004 006 001 14054
PART04found
GOOD RECORDPART04 LEFT FOOT REEBOKS             021 002 004 04323
PART06found
GOOD RECORDPART06 286 COMPUTERS W 4K HARD DISK  043 077 012 00042
```

27: VSAM Error Codes

VSAM file status codes in a COBOL program, and their meanings.
VSAM error codes which appear on the MVS job log and on the console.

VSAM File status codes in COBOL.

Sample program segments.

```
000100 FILE-CONTROL.
000200     SELECT VSAM-FILE ASSIGN VSAMFILE
000300          ORGANIZATION IS INDEXED
000400          ACCESS MODE  IS SEQUENTIAL
000500          RECORD KEY   IS VSAM-RECORD-KEY
000600          FILE STATUS  IS VSAM-STATUS-CODE
000700                          VSAM-EXTENDED-STATUS-CODE.
000800
000900 DATA DIVISION.
001000 FILE SECTION.
001100
001200 FD  VSAM-FILE.
001300 01  VSAM-RECORD.
001400     05  VSAM-RECORD-KEY         PIC X(20).
001500     05  VSAM-EMP-INFO           PIC X(60).
001600
001700 WORKING-STORAGE SECTION.
001800
001900 01  VSAM-STATUS-CODE.
002000     05 VSAM-STATUS-CODE-BYTE1    PIC X.
002100     05 VSAM-STATUS-CODE-BYTE2    PIC X.
002200
002300 01  VSAM-EXTENDED-STATUS-CODE.
002400     05 VSAM-EXTENDED-RETURN-CODE    PIC S9(4) COMP.
002500     05 VSAM-EXTENDED-FUNCTION-CODE PIC S9(4) COMP.
002600     05 VSAM-EXTENDED-FEEDBACK-CODE PIC S9(4) COMP.
002700
```

```
002800 EVALUATE-VSAM-STATUS-CODE.
002900*    THIS WILL DISPLAY DIAGNOSTIC MESSAGES
003000*    FOR VSAM STATUS CODES AS WELL AS ORDINARY SEQUENTIAL
003100     DISPLAY 'FILE STATUS CODE:' VSAM-STATUS-CODE
003200     EVALUATE VSAM-STATUS-CODE
003300     WHEN '00' DISPLAY 'SUCCESSFUL COMPLETION'
003400     WHEN '02' DISPLAY 'DUPLICATE KEY, NON UNIQ. ALT INDX'
003500     WHEN '04' DISPLAY 'READ, WRONG LENGTH RECORD'
003600     WHEN '05' DISPLAY 'OPEN, FILE NOT PRESENT'
003700     WHEN '07' DISPLAY 'CLOSE OPTION INCOMPAT FILE DEVICE'
003800              DISPLAY 'OPEN IMPLIES TAPE; TAPE NOT USED'
003900     WHEN '10' DISPLAY 'END OF FILE'
004000     WHEN '14' DISPLAY 'RRN > RELATIVE KEY DATA'
004100     WHEN '20' DISPLAY 'INVALID KEY VSAM KSDS OR RRDS'
004200     WHEN '21' DISPLAY 'SEQUENCE ERROR, ON WRITE'
004300              DISPLAY 'OR CHANGING KEY ON REWRITE'
004400     WHEN '22' DISPLAY 'DUPLICATE KEY'
004500     WHEN '23' DISPLAY 'RECORD OR FILE NOT FOUND'
004600     WHEN '24' DISPLAY 'BOUNDARY VIOLATION.'
004700              DISPLAY 'WRITE PAST END OF KSDS RECORD '
004800              DISPLAY 'COBOL 370: REL: REC# TOO BIG'
004900              DISPLAY 'OUT OF SPACE ON KSDS/RRDS FILE'
005000     WHEN '30' DISPLAY 'PERMANENT DATA ERROR'
005100              DISPLAY 'DATA CHECK, PARITY CHK, HARDW'
005200     WHEN '34' DISPLAY 'BOUNDARY VIOLATION'
005300              DISPLAY 'WRITE PAST END OF ESDS RECORD'
005400              DISPLAY 'OR NO SPACE TO ADD KSDS/RRDS RECORD'
005500              DISPLAY 'OUT OF SPACE ON SEQUENTIAL FILE'
005600     WHEN '35' DISPLAY 'OPEN, FILE NOT PRESENT'
005700     WHEN '37' DISPLAY 'OPEN MODE INCOMPAT WITH DEVICE'
005800     WHEN '38' DISPLAY 'OPENING FILE CLOSED WITH LOCK'
005900     WHEN '39' DISPLAY 'OPEN, FILE ATTRIB CONFLICTING'
006000     WHEN '41' DISPLAY 'OPEN, FILE IS OPEN'
006100     WHEN '42' DISPLAY 'CLOSE, FILE IS CLOSED'
006200     WHEN '43' DISPLAY 'DELETE OR REWRITE & NO GOOD READ FIRST'
006300     WHEN '44' DISPLAY 'BOUNDARY VIOLATION/REWRITE REC TOO BIG'
006400     WHEN '46' DISPLAY 'SEQUENTIAL READ WITHOUT POSITIONING'
006500     WHEN '47' DISPLAY 'READING FILE NOT OPEN AS INPUT/IO/EXTEND'
006600     WHEN '48' DISPLAY 'WRITE WITHOUT OPEN IO'
006700     WHEN '49' DISPLAY 'DELETE OR REWRITE WITHOUT OPEN IO'
006800     WHEN '90' DISPLAY 'UNKNOWN'
006900     WHEN '91' DISPLAY 'VSAM - PASSWORD FAILURE'
007000     WHEN '92' DISPLAY 'LOGIC ERROR/OPENING AN OPEN FILE'
007100              DISPLAY 'OR READING OUTPUT FILE'
007200              DISPLAY 'OR WRITE INPUT FILE'
007300              DISPLAY 'OR DEL/REW BUT NO PRIOR READ'
007400     WHEN '93' DISPLAY 'VSAM - VIRTSTOR. RESOURCE NOT AVAILABLE'
007500     WHEN '94' DISPLAY 'VSAM - SEQUENTIAL READ AFTER END OF FILE'
007600              DISPLAY 'OR NO CURRENT REC POINTER FOR SEQ'
007700     WHEN '95' DISPLAY 'VSAM - INVALID FILE INFORMATION'
007800              DISPLAY 'OR OPEN OUTPUT (LOAD) '
007900              DISPLAY   'WITH FILE THAT NEVER CONTNED DATA'
007910              DISPLAY   'OR ESDS OPEND OUTPUT BUT CONTNS DATA'
008000     WHEN '96' DISPLAY 'VSAM - MISSING DD STATEMENT IN JCL'
008100     WHEN '97' DISPLAY 'VSAM - OPEN OK, FILE INTEGRITY VERIFIED'
008200              DISPLAY 'FILE SHOULD BE OK'
008300     WHEN OTHER DISPLAY 'UNKNOWN REASON' VSAM-STATUS-CODE
008400     END-EVALUATE.
```

```
008900 EVALUATE-VSAM-EXTENDED-RETURN-CODE.
009000     EVALUATE VSAM-EXTENDED-RETURN-CODE
009100     WHEN 0 DISPLAY 'SUCCESSFUL COMPLETION'
009200     WHEN 4 DISPLAY 'ANOTHER REQUEST IS ACTIVE'
009300     WHEN 8 DISPLAY 'THERE IS A LOGICAL ERROR'
009400          PERFORM EVALUATE-LOGICAL-ERROR
009500     WHEN 12 DISPLAY 'THERE IS A PHYSICAL ERROR'
009600          PERFORM EVALUATE-PHYSICAL-ERROR
009700     WHEN OTHER DISPLAY 'UNKNOWN REASON'
009800     END-EVALUATE.
009900
010000 EVALUATE-VSAM-EXTENDED-FUNCTION-CODE.
010100     EVALUATE VSAM-EXTENDED-FUNCTION-CODE
010200     WHEN 0 DISPLAY 'ACCESSING BASE CLUSTER, NO PROBLEM'
010300     WHEN 1 DISPLAY 'ACCESSING BASE CLUSTER, MAY BE A PROBLEM'
010400     WHEN 2 DISPLAY 'ACCESSING ALTERNATE INDEX, NO PROBLEM'
010500     WHEN 3 DISPLAY 'ACCESSING ALTERNATE INDEX, MAY BE A PROBLEM'
010600     WHEN 4 DISPLAY 'UPGRADE PROCESSING, NO PROBLEM'
010700     WHEN 5 DISPLAY 'UPGRADE PROCESSING, MAY BE A PROBLEM'
010800     WHEN OTHER DISPLAY 'UNKNOWN REASON'
010900     END-EVALUATE.
011000
011100 EVALUATE-PHYSICAL-ERROR.
011200*    USE THIS WHEN THERE IS RC 12 IN VSAM-EXTENDED-RETURN-CODE
011300     EVALUATE VSAM-EXTENDED-FEEDBACK-CODE
011400     WHEN 4 DISPLAY 'READ ERROR ON DATA'
011500     WHEN 8 DISPLAY 'READ ERROR ON INDEX'
011600     WHEN 12 DISPLAY 'READ ERROR IN SEQUENCE SET'
011700     WHEN 16 DISPLAY 'WRITE ERROR ON DATA'
011800     WHEN 20 DISPLAY 'WRITE ERROR ON INDEX'
011900     WHEN 24 DISPLAY 'WRITE ERROR IN SEQUENCE SET'
012000     WHEN OTHER DISPLAY 'UNKNOWN REASON'
012100     END-EVALUATE.
012200
```

```
012300 EVALUATE-LOGICAL-ERROR.
012400*    USE THIS WHEN THERE IS RC  8 IN VSAM-EXTENDED-RETURN-CODE
012500     EVALUATE VSAM-EXTENDED-FEEDBACK-CODE
012600     WHEN   4 DISPLAY 'READ PAST END OF FILE'
012700     WHEN   8 DISPLAY 'DUPLICATE KEY'
012800     WHEN  12 DISPLAY 'KEY SEQUENCE ERROR'
012900     WHEN  16 DISPLAY 'NOT FOUND'
013000     WHEN  20 DISPLAY 'CONTROL INTERVAL IN USE BY OTHER JOB'
013100     WHEN  24 DISPLAY 'VOLUME CANNOT BE MOUNTED'
013200     WHEN  28 DISPLAY 'UNABLE TO EXTEND DATASET'
013300     WHEN  32 DISPLAY 'RBA NOT FOUND'
013400     WHEN  36 DISPLAY 'KEY IS NOT IN A DEFINED KEY RANGE'
013500     WHEN  40 DISPLAY 'INSUFFICIENT VIRTUAL STORAGE'
013600     WHEN  64 DISPLAY 'NO AVAILABLE STRINGS'
013700     WHEN  68 DISPLAY 'OPEN DID NOT SPECIFY PROC TYPE'
013800     WHEN  72 DISPLAY 'KEY ACCESS TO ESDS OR RRDS'
013900     WHEN  76 DISPLAY 'ATTEMPTED INSERT TO WRONG TYPE DATASET'
014000     WHEN  80 DISPLAY 'ATTEMPTED DELETE FROM ESDS'
014100     WHEN  84 DISPLAY 'OPTCD LOC FOR PUT REQUEST'
014200     WHEN  88 DISPLAY 'POSITION NOT ESTABLISHED'
014300     WHEN  92 DISPLAY 'PUT WITHOUT GET FOR UPDATE'
014400     WHEN  96 DISPLAY 'TRYING TO CHANGE PRIMARY KEY'
014500     WHEN 100 DISPLAY 'TRYING TO CHANGE LRECL'
014600     WHEN 104 DISPLAY 'INVALID RPL OPTIONS'
014700     WHEN 108 DISPLAY 'INVALID LRECL'
014800     WHEN 112 DISPLAY 'INVALID KEY LENGTH'
014900     WHEN 116 DISPLAY 'VIOLATED LOAD MODE RESTRICTION'
015000     WHEN 120 DISPLAY 'WRONG TASK SUBMITTING REQUEST'
015100     WHEN 132 DISPLAY 'TRYING TO GET SPANNED REC IN LOC MODE'
015200     WHEN 136 DISPLAY 'TRYING TO GET SPANNED REC BY ADDRESS'
015300            DISPLAY 'IN KSDS'
015400     WHEN 140 DISPLAY 'INCONSISTENT SPANNED REC'
015500     WHEN 144 DISPLAY 'ALT INDEX POINTER WITH NO MATCHING'
015600            DISPLAY 'BASE RECORD'
015700     WHEN 148 DISPLAY 'EXCEEDED MAX POINTERS IN ALT INDEX REC'
015800     WHEN 152 DISPLAY 'INSUFFICIENT BUFFERS AVAILABLE'
015900     WHEN 156 DISPLAY 'INVALID CONTROL INTERVAL'
016000     WHEN 192 DISPLAY 'INVALID RELATIVE REC NUMBER'
016100     WHEN 196 DISPLAY 'ATTEMPTED ADDRESSED REQUEST TO RRDS'
016200     WHEN 200 DISPLAY 'INVALID ACCESS THROUGH A PATH'
016300     WHEN 204 DISPLAY 'PUT IN BACKWARD MODE'
016400     WHEN 208 DISPLAY 'INVALID ENDREQ MACRO'
016500     WHEN OTHER DISPLAY 'UNKNOWN REASON'
016600     END-EVALUATE.
016700
```

27: VSAM Error Codes

VSAM Logical error codes
These codes indicate VSAM errors. They appear on the JOB log.

```
004(04)   Read past end of file
008(08)   You attempted to store a record with a Duplicate Key, or there
          is a duplicate record for an alternate index with unique key option.
012(0C)   You attempted to store a record out of Ascending Key Sequence
          in Skip-Sequential Mode; record had a Duplicate Key; for
          Skip-Sequential processing your GET, PUT, and POINT Requests
          are not referencing records in Ascending Sequence; or, for
          Skip-Sequential Retrieval, the key requested is lower than the
          previous key requested.  For Shared Resources, buffer pool is full.
016(10)   Record not found.
020(14)   Record already held in exclusive control by another requester.
024(18)   Record resides on a volume that cannot be mounted.
028(1C)   Data set cannot be extended because VSAM can't allocate additional
          Direct-Access Storage Space.  Either there is not enough space
          left to make the secondary allocation or you attempted to increase
          the size of a data set while processing SHROPT=4 and DISP=SHR.
036(24)   Key Ranges were specified for the data set when it was defined
          but no range was specified that includes the record to be inserted.
040(28)   Insufficient Virtual Storage to complete the request.
044(2A)   Work area too small.
064(40)   All available strings are in use.
068(44)   You attempted to use a type of processing (Output or Control-Interval
          Processing) that was not specified when the data set was opened.
074(4A)   Trying to use keys on ESDS or RRDS.
076(4C)   You issued an Addressed or Control-Interval PUT to add to a
          Key-Sequenced data set, or issued a Control-Interval put to a
          Relative Record data set.
080(50)   Trying to delete from ESDS.
084(54)   Using OPTCODE=LOC for a PUT.
088(58)   You issued a Sequential GET request without having caused VSAM
          to be positioned for it, or you changed from Addressed Access
          to Keyed Access without causing VSAM to be positioned for Keyed-
          Sequential Retrieval; there was no Sequential PUT insert for a
          Relative Record data set, or you attempted an illegal switch
          between forward and backward processing.
92(5C)    A PUT for update or an ERASE was issued without a previous GET
          for update, or a PUTIX was issued without a previous GETIX.
96(60)    Changing the Prime Key or Key of Reference when making an update.
100(64    Trying to change record length.
104(68)   The RPL options are either invalid or conflicting.
108(6C)   RECLEN specified was larger than the maximum allowed, equal to
          0, or smaller than the sum of the length and the displacement
          of the key field; RECLEN was not equal to record (SLOT) size
          specified for a Relative Record data set.
```

27: VSAM Error Codes

```
112(70)   Invalid key length.
116(74)   Trying to update an empty dataset.
120(78)   Request was submitted by the wrong task.
132(84)   An attempt was made in Locate Mode to retrieve a Spanned Record.
136(88)   You attempted an Addressed GET of a Spanned record in a KSDS set.
140(8C)   Inconsistent Spanned record.
144(90)   Invalid pointer (no associated base record) in an Alternate Index.
148(94)   Maximum number of Alternate Index pointers exceeded.
152(98)   Not enough buffers available.
156(9C)   Invalid control interval.
192(C0)   Invalid Relative Record number in a RRDS dataset.
196(C4)   Addressed access to a Relative Record (RRDS) dataset is not allowed.
200(C8)   Addressed access/Generic Backwrd processng by Key thru path  not allowed
204(CC)   Attempting a PUT in backward mode.
252(FC)   Record mode processing is not allowed for a Linear data set.
```

27: VSAM Error Codes

VSAM Open error codes

136(88) Not enough Virtual-Storage Space is available for Work Areas, Control Blocks, or Buffers.

144(90) An uncorrectable I/O error occurred while VSAM was Reading or Writing a catalog record.

148(94) No record for the data set to be opened was found in the available catalog(s) or an unidentified error occurred while VSAM was searching the catalog.

152(98) Security Verification failed; the password specified in the Access-Method Control Block for a specified level of access does not match the password in the catalog for that level of access.

164(A4) An uncorrectable I/O error occurred while VSAM was Reading the Volume Label.

168(A8) The data set is not available for the type of processing you specify, or an attempt was made to open a Reusable data set with the Reset option while another user had the data set.

176(B0) An error occurred while VSAM was attempting to fix a page of Virtual storage in Real storage.

180(B4) A VSAM catalog specified in JCL either does not exist or is not open, and no record for the data set to be opened was found in any other catalog.

184(B8) An uncorrectable I/O error occurred while VSAM was completing an I/O request.

188(BC) The data set indicated by the Access-Method Control Block is not of the type that may be specified by an Access-Method Control Block.

192(C0) An unusable data set was opened for output.

232(E8) Reset was specified for a nonreusable data set and the data set is not empty.

236(EC) A permanent Staging error occurred in MSS (Acquire).

244(F4) The Volume containing the Catalog Recovery area was not mounted and verified for output processing.

This page intentionally left blank

Appendix.

When uploading, remember that most upload utilities require you to specify ASCII conversion (I.E. convert ASCII to EBCDIC) and CRLF (Carriage Return, Line Feed.)

After you upload the files and programs install the files in the following suggested way.

A. Create a PDS/PDSE (partitioned dataset) according to company standards that will hold the COBOL programs. A typical name would be: *userid*.COBBOOK.COBOL.

B. Place each model program into this COBOL library, as a member. Use the same names I've used in this book, for example: SEQSIMP1. The file and member names would be: *userid*.COBBOOK.COBOL(SEQSIMP1).

C. Create a PDS/PDSE according to company standards that will hold the data files. A typical name would be: *userid*.COBBOOK.DATA.

D. Place each data file into this DATA PDS/PDSE, as a member. Use the same names I've used in this book, for example: PARTS1.
The file and member names would be: *userid*.COBBOOK.DATA(PARTS1).

E. Create a PDS/PDSE (partitioned dataset) according to company standards that will hold the sample JCL.
A typical name would be: *userid*.COBBOOK.CNTL.
Put the JCL files into this .CNTL library, as members.

G. The JCL to create the VSAM files in included at the end of the chapters where it is needed. Modify it according to your company's standards, and for the data set name of the data file that will be input to the utility that creates the VSAM file.

H. The following pages will assist in verifying if you have transferred the data correctly.

Some programming suggestions for COBOL.
Open data files at the logical beginning of the program. You must specify INPUT, OUTPUT, or IO. Close those files just before ending the program. That assures file integrity.
If the program terminates abnormally, you will not have a chance to close the files, but the operating system will close them. But since the program didn't work, the output files created by your program should not be considered reliable.

Appendix.

Verifying the uploaded data.
You should have transferred the required data files and placed them into *userid*.COBBOOK.DATA.
You should have the following members in *userid*.COBBOOK.DATA, containing the data that is
shown here. A two-line column ruler precedes the data.

userid.COBBOOK.DATA(EMP)
Used in programs SEQCK1, SELECT1, BINSRCH1.
```
          1         2         3         4         5         6
123456789.123456789.123456789.123456789.123456789.123456789.12345678
        01000  PEARLE E GATES             D0001 01
        02000  LED BALOON                 D0002 04
        03000  ORTIZ, DAVID               D0005 06
        04000  JOE JONES                  D0504 01
```

userid.COBBOOK.DATA(EMPNAMES)
Used in program VSAMRND2.
```
          1         2         3         4         5         6
123456789.123456789.123456789.123456789.123456789.123456789.12345678
BUD WEIZER            YUP, HE S THERE
PHIL HARMONIC         OK
L. A. CALIFORNIA      OK TOO
HERB GARDNER          CALLING ALL GREEN THUMBS
HAL A. PENO           THIS ISN T THERE (TRY TACO BELL)
```

userid.COBBOOK.DATA(EMPSORTD)
Used in an IDCAMS to create VSAM file as input to program VSAMSEQ1 (optionally VSAMSEQ2),
VSAMRND1, VSAMRND2, VSAMLOD1, VSAMACD1, VSAMSTR1.
```
          1         2         3         4         5         6
123456789.123456789.123456789.123456789.123456789.123456789.12345678

BUD WEIZER            05000  9  0001  0000001  000000
HERB GARDNER          03000  1  0040  0000055  000022
HUGH MUNGUS           06000  1  0200  0000020  000020
L. A. CALIFORNIA      07000  5  0020  0000033  000033
PAT SULLIVAN          04000  0  0002  0000022  000011
PEARLE E. GATES       01000  2  0010  0000020  000300
PHIL HARMONIC         02000  3  0030  0000050  000020
```

userid.COBBOOK.DATA(EMPTRANS)
Used in program VSAMACD1.

```
          1         2         3         4         5         6
123456789.123456789.123456789.123456789.123456789.123456789.12345678
A   ALLEN ROENTCH        05000  9  0001  0000001  000000
C   HERB GARDNER         03000  1  0040  0000055  000022
D   HUGH MUNGUS          06000  1  0200  0000020  000020
A   L. A. CALIFORNIA     07000  5  0020  0000033  000033
C   LISA CARR            04000  0  0002  0000022  000011
D   MAL A. MUTE          01000  2  0010  0000020  000300
X   PHIL HARMONIC        02000  3  0030  0000050  000020
```

userid.COBBOOK.DATA(EMP1)
Used in program VALID1.

```
          1         2         3         4         5         6
123456789.123456789.123456789.123456789.123456789.123456789.12345678
          00001 ZONE, CAL               D0001 01
          00002 RAMIREZ, MANNY          D0004 02
          00003 PEDD, MOE               D0003 04
          00004 MANDER, SAL A.          D0029 09
          00005 BEARER, PAUL            D0003 03
          00006 AARON, HANK             D0003 01
          00025 COBB, TY                D0022 24
          00032 BONDS, BARRY            D0008 23
          00041 YONARA, CY              D0004 22
          00051 DEAN, JAMES             D0002 13
          00054 GATOR, AL E.            D0005 07
          00056 TYME, JUSTIN            D0004 08
          00057 CASE, JUSTIN            D0004 03
          01000 PEARLE E GATES          D0001 01
```

userid.COBBOOK.DATA(EMP2)
Used in programs DIRSUB1, SERSRCH1, BINSRCH1.

```
          1         2         3         4         5         6
123456789.123456789.123456789.123456789.123456789.123456789.12345678
          01000 PEARLE E GATES          D0001 01 05
          02000 LED BALOON              D0002 04 09
          03000 ORTIZ, DAVID            D0005 06 01
          04000 JOE JONES               D0504 01 12
```

Appendix.

userid.COBBOOK.DATA(FIXEDINP)
Used in programs VARWRIT1, VARODOW1.
```
          1         2         3         4         5         6
123456789.123456789.123456789.123456789.123456789.123456789.12345678
MEDIUM    BETH      KELLY     ANTHONY
LONG      LAURA     RICK      NANCY     MARIA     ELLEN
SHORT     MOE
MEDIUM    NORMA     DENISE    JEAN
LONG      MAURA     NICK      SALLY     MARIO     ELLIE
```

userid.COBBOOK.DATA(OLDMAST)
Used in program FILEUPD1.
```
          1         2         3         4         5         6
123456789.123456789.123456789.123456789.123456789.123456789.12345678
ACCT0     00010     LOU       OLDMAST
ACCT1     00010     MOE       OLDMAST
ACCT2     00010     CURLY     OLDMAST
ACCT3     00010     HAPPY     OLDMAST
ACCT5     00010     LAUREL    OLDMAST
ACCT6     00010     HARDY     OLDMAST
ACCT8     00010     DUMBO     OLDMAST
ACCT9     00010     GEORGE    OLDMAST
```

userid.COBBOOK.DATA(PARTS)
Used in programs SEQSIMP1, SEQRPT1, SEQRPT2.
```
          1         2         3         4         5         6
123456789.123456789.123456789.123456789.123456789.123456789.12345678
PART01  LEFT HANDED WIDGET WRENCHES     003 007 002 10022
PART02  LEAD-WINGED GLIDERS             004 006 001 14054
PART04  LEFT FOOT REEBOKS               021 002 004 04323
PART06  286 COMPUTERS W 4K HARD DISK    043 077 012 00042
```

userid.COBBOOK.DATA(PARTS1)
Used in programs EVAL1, LOADTBL2, LOADODO1.
```
          1         2         3         4         5         6
123456789.123456789.123456789.123456789.123456789.123456789.12345678
PART01                                  003 007 002 10022
PART02                                  004 006 001 14054
PART04                                  021 002 004 04323
PART06                                  043 077 012 00042
```

Appendix.

userid.COBBOOK.DATA(PARTTABL)
Used in programs LOADTBL1, LOADTBL2, LOADODO1.

```
          1         2         3         4         5         6
123456789.123456789.123456789.123456789.123456789.123456789.12345678
PART01 LEFT HANDED WIDGET WRENCHES
PART02 LEAD-WINGED GLIDERS
PART04 LEFT FOOT REEBOKS
PART06 286 COMPUTERS W 4K HARD DISK
```

userid.COBBOOK.DATA(SALES1)
Used in program BRKLV1.

```
          1         2         3         4         5         6
123456789.123456789.123456789.123456789.123456789.123456789.12345678
CT    HARTFORD   ANN SAMUELS      CHEVELLE         000800000
CT    HARTFORD   THIERRY HENRI    FERRARI          006000000
CT    NEW HAVEN  ANNA JONES       OMNI             000030000
CT    NEW HAVEN  ANNA JONES       STING RAY        000200000
CT    NEW HAVEN  ANNA JONES       STING RAY        000200000
CT    NEW HAVEN  ANNA JONES       STING RAY        000200000
CT    NEW HAVEN  JETER, DEREK     CAMARO           000600000
CT    NEW HAVEN  CAL ZONI         JAGUAR           009000000
CT    NEW HAVEN  CAL ZONI         PEUGEOT          000200000
CT    NEW HAVEN  ROSE BUSH        PINTO            000040000
MA    BOSTON     JOE JONES        HONDA            000010000
MA    BOSTON     RON ZONEY        LEMON            000020000
MA    BOSTON     RON ZONEY        SUBARU           000010000
MI    DETROIT    CAM NEWTON       EDSEL            000000010
MI    DETROIT    CAM NEWTON       FIAT             004000000
MI    DETROIT    CAM NEWTON       FORD             000020000
MI    DETROIT    CAM NEWTON       STUDEBAKER       000000600
NY    ALBANY     JERRY RICE       CONTINENTAL      002000000
NY    ALBANY     JERRY RICE       ESCORT           000010000
NY    ALBANY     JERRY RICE       FORD             000010000
NY    ALBANY     JERRY RICE       HYUNDAI          000010000
NY    ALBANY     JERRY RICE       HYUNDAI          000010000
NY    ROCHESTER  BILL E. GOAT     MASERATI         000001000
```

Appendix.

***userid*.COBBOOK.DATA(SALES3)**
Used in program BRKLV3.

```
          1         2         3         4         5         6
123456789.123456789.123456789.123456789.123456789.123456789.12345678
CT   HARTFORD   ANN SAMUELS        CHEVELLE          000800000
CT   HARTFORD   THIERRY HENRI      FERRARI           006000000
CT   NEW HAVEN  ANNA JONES         OMNI              000030000
CT   NEW HAVEN  ANNA JONES         STING RAY         000200000
CT   NEW HAVEN  ANNA JONES         STING RAY         000200000
CT   NEW HAVEN  ANNA JONES         STING RAY         000200000
CT   NEW HAVEN  JETER, DEREK       CAMARO            000600000
CT   NEW HAVEN  CAL ZONI           JAGUAR            009000000
CT   NEW HAVEN  CAL ZONI           PEUGEOT           000200000
CT   NEW HAVEN  ROSE BUSH          PINTO             000040000
MA   BOSTON     JOE JONES          HONDA             000010000
MA   BOSTON     RON ZONEY          LEMON             000020000
MA   BOSTON     RON ZONEY          SUBARU            000010000
MI   DETROIT    CAM NEWTON         EDSEL             000000010
MI   DETROIT    CAM NEWTON         FIAT              004000000
MI   DETROIT    CAM NEWTON         FORD              000020000
MI   DETROIT    CAM NEWTON         STUDEBAKER        000000600
NY   ALBANY     JERRY RICE         CONTINENTAL       002000000
NY   ALBANY     JERRY RICE         ESCORT            000010000
NY   ALBANY     JERRY RICE         FORD              000010000
NY   ALBANY     JERRY RICE         HYUNDAI           000010000
NY   ALBANY     JERRY RICE         HYUNDAI           000010000
NY   ROCHESTER  BILL E. GOAT       MASERATI          000001000
```

Appendix.

userid.COBBOOK.DATA(TRANSFIL)
Used in program FILEUPD1.

```
          1         2         3         4         5         6
123456789.123456789.123456789.123456789.123456789.123456789.12345678
ACCT0     00100     GRUMPY    CHANGE       TRANSFIL
ACCT1     00100     SNEAZZY   ADD          TRANSFIL
ACCT1     00100     RUDOLPH   CHANGE       TRANSFIL
ACCT1     00100               DELETE       TRANSFIL
ACCT2     00100     BLITZEN   CHANGE       TRANSFIL
ACCT4     00100     THUMPER   ADD          TRANSFIL
ACCT5     00100               DELETE       TRANSFIL
ACCT7     00100     MR ED     ADD          TRANSFIL
ACCT8     00100     DONNER    CHANGE       TRANSFIL
ACCT8     00100     WIMPY     CHANGE       TRANSFIL
ACCT9     00100     TOTO      CHANGE       TRANSFIL
```

userid.COBBOOK.DATA(UNSORTED)
Used in program SORTEX1.

```
          1         2         3         4         5         6
123456789.123456789.123456789.123456789.123456789.123456789.12345678
ACCT0     00100     GRUMPY    CHANGE       TRANSFIL
ACCT8     00100     WIMPY     CHANGE       TRANSFIL
ACCT1     00100     SNEAZZY   ADD          TRANSFIL
ACCT1     00100     SNEAZZY   ADD          TRANSFIL
ACCT1     00100     RUDOLPH   CHANGE       TRANSFIL
ACCT1     00100               DELETE       TRANSFIL
ACCT4     00100     THUMPER   ADD          TRANSFIL
ACCT5     00100               DELETE       TRANSFIL
ACCT7     00100     MR ED     ADD          TRANSFIL
ACCT8     00100     DONNER    CHANGE       TRANSFIL
ACCT9     00100     TOTO      CHANGE       TRANSFIL
```

Appendix.

The VSAM files.
After uploading the data and placing it in the appropriate PDS/PDSE with the member name that is shown, you can create the VSAM files.

userid.VSAMKSDS.EMPSORTD
The data that is input to IDCAMS which creates *userid*.**VSAMKSDS.EMPSORTD**
userid.COBBOOK.DATA(EMPSORTD)
This VSAM file is used by programs **VSAMLOD1, VSAMSEQ1, VSAMSEQ2(optional), VSAMRND1, VSAMLOD1, VSAMACD1, VSAMSTR1**

```
//* vsamseq1.jcl
//DEFKSDS  EXEC PGM=IDCAMS
//SYSPRINT DD   SYSOUT=*
//SYSIN    DD   *
 DELETE (userid.VSAMKSDS.EMPSORTD) CLUSTER

 DEFINE CLUSTER -
 (NAME(userid.VSAMKSDS.EMPSORTD) -
  CYLINDERS(1,1) -
  KEYS(20,0) -
  RECORDSIZE(80,80) -
  VOLUMES(insert a volume serial number here) -
  INDEXED )

 REPRO INFILE(INFILE) OUTDATASET(userid.VSAMKSDS.EMPSORTD)

/*
//INFILE DD   DSN=userid.COBBOOK.DATA(EMPSORTD),DISP=SHR
//*
//STEP1    EXEC PGM=VSAMSEQ1
//STEPLIB DD DSN=your.executable.program.library.here,DISP=SHR
//*   THE NEXT DATASET NAME MAY BE DIFFERENT AT YOUR CO
//VSAMKSDS   DD   DSN=userid.VSAMKSDS.EMPSORTD,DISP=SHR
//SYSOUT     DD   SYSOUT=*
//SYSUDUMP   DD   SYSOUT=*
//SYSABOUT   DD   SYSOUT=*
//SYSDBOUT   DD   SYSOUT=*
//*
```

The VSAM files, continued.

userid.VSAMKSDS.NOTLOADD.EMPSORTD

This is created EMPTY. Data is loaded into it by program VSAMLOD1.

```
//* vsamlod1.jcl
//DEFKSDS   EXEC PGM=IDCAMS
//SYSPRINT DD    SYSOUT=*
//SYSIN     DD    *
 DELETE (userid.VSAMKSDS.NOTLOADD.EMPSORTD) CLUSTER

 DEFINE CLUSTER -
 (NAME(userid.VSAMKSDS.NOTLOADD.EMPSORTD) -
  CYLINDERS(1,1) -
  KEYS(20,0) -
  RECORDSIZE(80,80) -
  VOLUMES(insert a volume serial number here) -
  INDEXED )
/*
//*
```

By the same author

Revised Apr5 2024 12

The REXX Language on TSO
ISBN-10: 1479104779, ISBN-13: 978-1479104772   (Published September 5, 2012)
How to use REXX to program on z/OS TSO/ISPF.

The REXX Language on TSO: REXX Functions   (Published July 13, 2013)
ISBN-10: 1490536078, ISBN-13: 978-1490536071
The built-in functions that are an integral part of the REXX language.

TSO CLIST to TSO REXX: Conversion Handbook
ISBN-10: 1508668493, ISBN-13: 978-1508668497   (Published May 1, 2015)
If you are converting CLIST programs to REXX, you will find this book useful.

Legacy Languages: Model COBOL programs with logic examples.
ISBN-13: 979-8694086097
Actual programs you can use as a model to create programs to solve common business programming problems.

Italian Dialogues: Learn Italian by Speaking Italian
ISBN-13: 979-8607849764   (Published August 10, 2020)

Italian Pronunciation
ISBN-13: 978-1976097997
ISBN-10: 1976097991   (Published June 27, 2018)

ESL: 17 Student Questions Answered
Clear answers to questions posed by students in ESL class.
ISBN-13: 978-1721980390
ISBN-10: 1721980393   (Published July 27, 2018)

French Expressions
Popular French expressions explained.
ISBN-13: 978-1489573476
ISBN-10: 148957347X   (Published June 9, 2013)
Kindle Edition: ASIN: B008UDGCZ6

Idiotismes, locutions, et expressions américains
Popular American expressions explained, and translated into French.
(French Edition)
By Gabriel F. Gargiulo
ISBN-13: 978-1490495583 ISBN-10: 1490495584   (Published June 29, 2013)
Kindle Edition: ASIN: B008PX0SWO   (Published July 26, 2012)